WHEN YOU WORK FOR A BULLY

WHEN YOU WORK FOR A BULLY
Assessing Your Options and Taking Action

Susan Futterman

Croce Publishing Group, LLC
Montvale, New Jersey

Published in 2004 by Croce Publishing Group, LLC
PO Box 339, Montvale, NJ 07645-0339
(201) 248-3175, (201) 802-9353 (Fax), info@crocepublishing.com

Distributed by Independent Publishers Group
814 North Franklin St. Chicago, IL 60610
(800) 888-4741, (312) 337-5985 (Fax), orders@ipgbook.com

First Edition

Library of Congress Cataloging-in-Publication Data

Futterman, Susan.
  When you work for a bully: assessing your options and taking action /
by Susan Futterman.
     p. cm.
ISBN 0-9719538-8-0 (pbk.: alk. paper)
1. Bullying in the workplace. 2. Harassment.
3. Managing your boss.
I. Title.
HF5549.5.E43F88 2004
650.1'3--dc22

                                                              2003022738

Printed in the United States of America

CONTENTS

FOREWORD

This book is dedicated to my husband Fred Paroutaud and my parents Ed and Shirley Futterman, in appreciation for their loving and unconditional support; to my good friends, Kelly Snow and Debby Nichols; and to my three cats (in alphabetical order) Amelia, Nadia and Prudence, whose silliness makes so much endurable.

I would also like to thank the many people who have helped me, not only with this book but to recover from my own experience with working for a bully. My appreciation goes out to (again in alphabetical order) Edward Beck, EdD, CCMHC, NCC, LPC; David Bowman; Paul Buchanan, JD; Margy Cassidy; Tom Davison, MA, PhD, CFP™; Michael Dubis, CFP™, Eileen Freiberger, CFP™; Tim Field; Gerriann Fox; Harvey Hornstein, PhD; Lana Kapchinsky; Chris Long, CFP™; Dori Miller; Steve Murphy, JD; Gary Namie, PhD; Joel Neuman, PhD; Chris Nordgren, PhD; Don Sessions, JD; Laura Sofield, MSN, APRN, BC; Michael Sorgen, JD; Don Spero, JD; James Stoneman, JD; Becky W.; David Yamada, JD; and others, who provided me with valuable insights and information, as well as to the members of the Toxic Managers and Healing Work online groups.

And, to the man who made it all possible, my very own bully. If you're reading this, then you know who you are. Stand up and take a bow.

INTRODUCTION

So much of what we call management consists in making it difficult for people to work.
—*Peter F. Drucker, from* Peter's Quotations: Ideas for Our Times

"Management" means, in the last analysis, the substitution of thought for brawn and muscle, of knowledge for folklore and superstition, and of cooperation for force.
—*Peter F. Drucker, from* People and Performance: The Best of Peter F. Drucker on Management

An occasional run-in, or perhaps even an outright argument, with your employer is not unusual. It in fact may be positive, clearing the air and helping you both to get off to a new start. But when the confrontations become constant, bitter and, ultimately, abusive, it's time to take action.

Since you are reading this book, you've probably already recognized the bully in your life and are attempting to deal with him or her (Bullies are just as likely to be male as female, just as targets may be either male or female. For the sake of simplicity, I've used the male pronoun throughout this book.).

Information on coping strategies and on attempting to lessen the abuse is readily available. But what happens when you no longer want to play the game, when you are no longer willing to give up part of your soul in order to keep your paycheck? How can you move on emotionally, financially and professionally?

If you are the target of a workplace bully, who also happens to be your manager, this book provides the information you need to make the best possible choices about your future.

If you're not quite sure what the phrase "bullying in the workplace" actually means, and whether it describes your own situation, *When You Work for a Bully* will help you to crystallize your situation and, if you are seeking a new job, will help you avoid signing up a second time with a potentially "toxic," or abusive, boss.

Targets of workplace bullies often find themselves in a sort of limbo. Toxic managers may be verbally abusive, highly manipulative or just plain bullies. However, if the harassment cannot be linked to a specific protected class (for example, race or gender), then the manager's behavior is probably technically legal if nonetheless obnoxious. In some states, however, lawmakers are now considering making a change; more on that later. For the most part, however, you will probably not have the usual legal remedies at hand. And before you turn to the courts for a decision, you need to be aware of the pitfalls you may encounter. These are examined later in this book.

At the same time, you may be well-advised to look closely at your bully's motivation. As you do so, you may discover a pattern that indicates his bullying does indeed violate existing law—or that his treatment of you is retaliatory in nature and, again, may be illegal (See Chapter 8, "Bullying and the Law.").

In *Violence at Work*, published in 1998, the International Labour Organization, an agency of the United Nations, called bullying, which it defines as "offensive behavior through vindictive, cruel, malicious or humiliating attempts to undermine an individual or groups of employees," one of the fastest growing components of workplace violence.

In his book, *Brutal Bosses and Their Prey*, Harvey Hornstein estimated that as many as 20 million Americans face workplace abuse on a daily basis. The toll that verbal abuse takes on the victim runs the gamut from strained relations with friends and family, panic and anxiety attacks, severe depression and, at the extreme end of the spectrum, to suicide and/or homicide.

In this book, you'll learn what you can do to avoid those catastrophic effects and transition into a new life.

ON THE NOMENCLATURE

Many anti-bully advocates oppose, on a variety of grounds, the use of the word "victim" in connection with those who are bullied.

Some believe there is a need to distinguish between those who have been subjected to physical abuse (victims) as opposed to non-physical abuse. Others contend that the word "victim" triggers preconceived notions about the nature of victims, leading the observer to conclude that the bullied person has somehow brought the bullying on himself.

In contrast, in the following pages, "victim" is used essentially interchangeably with the word "target," a decision based on the third definition provided in *Webster's New World Dictionary*. Here are all three definitions of victim:

1. a person or animal killed as a sacrifice to a god in a religious rite

2. someone or something killed, destroyed, injured, or otherwise harmed by, or suffering from, some act, condition, or circumstance [victims of war]

3. a person who suffers some loss, especially by being swindled

Bullying fits this third definition well. Bullies cheat those they target out of the dignity and respect to which they are entitled. They swindle their victims out of self-esteem, confidence, and happiness.

1.

WHAT IS WORKPLACE BULLYING?

This book comes out of my own experience with a workplace bully—my former boss. Up until I met him, I was confident in my ability to do my job, believed I had reasonably good people skills, and was a conscientious, responsible and valuable employee. Up to that time, my performance evaluations and letters of recommendation from various past employers had confirmed those assumptions. But in this particular position, I was outmatched.

In less than six months, I was a wreck. I was working 12-hour days, with an increasing number of those hours devoted to responding to the continuing barrage of memos, emails, and voice-mails criticizing my performance. Every time the phone rang, I jumped; every time a new email appeared on my computer screen, I cringed in anticipation of yet another twist of the knife.

Panic attacks became part of my life, although it took me awhile before I recognized them for what they were. My hands, my arms, my whole body would tremble. I couldn't breathe; my heart would pound. At night, I would go home and cry. And, increasingly I would cry at work, especially after a particularly nasty encounter. Most of the time I would cry in my office but sometimes, to my chagrin, I would break down in front of my colleagues.

My husband was worried; he wanted me to resign. I kept thinking that somehow I could get through to my manager, that we could resolve the issues and that, finally, we would all live happily ever after.

Of course, that never happened. Instead, I reached the breaking point. The doctor I had recently started seeing insisted that, one way or another, I stop going to work, at least for awhile. Finally, and sometimes, I think, just in time, I did. Never, for a single moment have I regretted it. I only regret that it took me so long.

Bullying may be defined as using one's authority to undermine, frighten or intimidate another person, often leaving the victim feeling afraid, powerless, incompetent and ashamed. In the workplace, bullying is characterized by a wide array of behaviors, from subtle to glaringly obvious.

Often the targets of bullies enjoy their work, or would, if left alone to do it. But once targeted by a bully, they are faced with increasingly unreasonable demands and a constant campaign to undermine them until they are finally forced either to quit or call for help. Frequently the effort of the bully to undermine includes humiliating the target; diminishing the individual's authority and autonomy; overloading the individual with work or, conversely, taking away the usual workload and replacing it with menial and/or meaningless tasks; constant, unnecessary oversight; and distorting or even fabricating "facts" relating to the target's performance.

Bullying often begins in a relatively subtle fashion and almost always represents an accumulation of many seemingly minor events. That makes it even more insidious because events, when taken in isolation and out of context, may seem trivial. It may take weeks, even months, for targets of bullies to realize that they are being bullied.

Indeed, victims often unwittingly contribute to that delay in understanding what is happening to them. They typically have high standards themselves, have done well at their jobs in the past, have consistently received above-average performance evaluations and are dedicated to their work. It is these very qualities that make the victims easy targets, since they are typically eager, and sometimes over-eager, to please their managers. They want to do their job well and they take pride in their work. When they encounter the initial swells of criticism, they redouble their efforts: working harder, staying later, and doing more, but to no avail.

If you find that you're abruptly excluded from meetings that you habitually attended in the past and/or that you need to attend in order to do your job, if your manager subjects you to persistent and unwarranted criticism whether public or private, and if your manager undercuts your authority and/or areas of responsibility, you are being bullied. Similarly, if your manager constantly condescends to or patronizes you, withholds information you need to do your job, constantly and arbitrarily changes your work deadlines, and bombards you with memos and telephone calls focused on minutiae, you can be be pretty certain that you've been targeted by a bully. Conversely, if your bully refuses to return your calls or respond to your memos, ignores or constantly interrupts your work or comments or denigrates you to coworkers or clients, you can again be pretty certain that you've been targeted by a bully.

In addition to an intense focus on the trivial, bullying is often also characterized by a constant refusal to recognize the target's positive contributions, achievements, or intrinsic value. Your work is never quite good enough. If forced to say something positive about your work, your manager will almost always accompany the reluctant compliment with a derogatory comment.

If you're a manager yourself, you've probably learned to temper constructive criticism with positive feedback in order to avoid discouraging your staff. If you're a bully, you'll do the opposite. For example, criticism from a "negative" manager, whether a bully, or simply a poor communicator (See Chapter 3, "Profile of a Target" for a discussion on distinguishing the two.), might sound something like this: "You did a good job with this project, too bad you don't show the same commitment to the work you're supposed to be focusing on." Or: "I appreciate your staying late to get this project out on time. Now, in the future, if you could just be more organized."

Of course, there is the possibility that you did put extra effort into a special project or that maybe you could stand to organize your time a little bit better. Only you can put such comments into their proper context.

But even if criticism were in order, it could be phrased differently. If your manager is trying to motivate, rather than intimidate, you might instead hear something like: "You did a good job on this assignment. Let's figure out how to apply some of the skills and talents you've demonstrated here to other projects." Or: "I appreciate your staying late to get this project out on time. When the deadline is over, let's sit down and talk about what we might be able to change, so that no one will need to stay late the next time around."

If whatever you do is not good enough, if you're constantly singled out for criticism over trivia, if you feel you are doing a good job and that your boss is unable to or unwilling to recognize it, then you have a problem that, one way, or another, you need to resolve.

Clearly, bullying in the workplace is many things, often obnoxious, frequently cruel. What it is not, however, is illegal in the US, unless it devolves even further into physical violence and/or is directed against members of protected classes identified by laws such as Title VII of the Civil Rights Act of 1964 or subsequent federal measures, such as the Americans with Disabilities Act (ADA) and the Age Discrimination in Employment Act (ADEA).

"EQUAL OPPORTUNITY" BULLYING

Title VII of the Civil Rights Act of 1964 makes it illegal for any employer to "fail or refuse to hire or to discharge any individual, or otherwise to discriminate against any individual with respect to his compensation, terms, conditions, or privileges of employment, because of such individual's race, color, religion, sex, or national origin."

As this book went to press, there was no law on the books on either the federal or state level dealing with "equal-opportunity bullying," also known as "nonspecific harassment." However, as discussed in Chapter 17, "Legal Directions," legislative measures have been introduced in California and Oregon that would extend protection to nonspecific harassment. Unfortunately, both measures appear to be stagnating.

Certainly, bullying seems pervasive enough to justify such legislation. According to a number of studies, workplace bullying is extraordinarily common. For example, a 1999 Wayne State University study found bullying to be an experience that four out of five employees—23 million people in the United States—will deal with at some point during their careers.

Although not all of these individuals will face bullying dramatic enough to cause them severe stress, much less to force them out of their jobs, thousands, if not millions, of them will find their lives change dramatically for the worse because of the bullying they confront.

Other classic behaviors of the bully include denying targets the training they need, refusing employees leave they've earned and requiring their victims to meet unrealistic goals and deadlines that change as they approach them.

Because bullying frequently takes the form of cumulative events that, in isolation, could be considered minor, neither victims of bullying nor their coworkers may be aware that such behavior is in fact taking place. And employees struggle to meet objectives that either can never be met or, when met, will change once again.

Although many targets of bullying tend to rationalize, and thus to minimize, the impact of the abuse on them, a 1998 report on workplace violence released by the UK's International Labour Organization (ILO) concluded that physical and emotional violence is one of the most serious problems facing the 21st century workplace.

The ILO definition of workplace violence includes bullying, which it describes in *Violence at Work* as "any incident in which a person is abused, threatened or assaulted in circumstances relating to their work. These behaviors may originate from customers or from coworkers at any level of the organization. This definition would include all forms of harassment, bullying, intimidation, physical threats/assaults, robbery, and other intrusive behaviors."

According to the ILO, employees expressing concerns about inappropriate, unethical or bullying behaviors are frequently stigmatized as having a negative attitude, being paranoid or engaging in whistle blowing.

US psychologist and author Gary Namie contends that bullying represents a significant health hazard to the person targeted. According to a 2000 survey conducted by Namie's Workplace Bullying & Trauma Institute, of those targeted by bullies:

· Forty-one percent were diagnosed with depression.

· More than 80 percent reported effects that prevented them from being productive at work (severe anxiety, lost concentration, sleeplessness, etc.).

· Post-traumatic stress disorder (PTSD) affected 31 percent of the women and 21 percent of men.

These, and other health impacts of the workplace bully are discussed further in Chapter 4, "Impact of Bullying."

BULLIES IN ALL PROFESSIONS

Unfortunately no aspect of American society appears to be safe from the workplace bully—certainly not the healthcare sector.

In 1991, Helen Cox, EdD, MSN, RN, surveyed hundreds of nurses about their experiences with verbal abuse. In 1999, Laura Sofield, MSN, APRN, BC, conducted a similar study. Both researchers found that more than 90 percent of nurses they surveyed had experienced verbal abuse, and most encountered an average of five incidents per month.

"EXPLORING PERSISTENT PATTERNS OF WORKPLACE AGGRESSION"

According to "Exploring Persistent Patterns of Workplace Aggression," by Loraleigh Keashly and Joel H. Neuman, the following frequencies of workplace aggression are experienced by the corresponding percentages of people in the workplace:

- no aggression: five percent
- less than once weekly: 58 percent
- one to five events weekly: 29 percent
- at least six events weekly: seven percent

The majority of respondents in both studies named physicians as the most common perpetrators. And in both surveys, the majority of nurses said that the abuse increased turnover rates and contributed to the nursing shortage. Many also reported that such abuse tended to increase the number of errors on the job.

In an article written for *Surgical Services Management* in June 2000, Sofield, together with Carrie Lybecker, RN, noted that verbal abuse is not only pervasive in the medical professions, but it has a lasting impact, with some nurses reporting that previous verbal abuse still affects them 20 or more years later.

More recently, Sofield, along with Susan Salmond, EdD, RN, CNAA, in "Workplace Violence," an analysis of abusive behaviors in hospitals published in the July/August 2003 issue of *Orthopaedic Nursing*, found that 91 percent of the respondents in a subsequent study had experienced verbal abuse in the prior month. Although some of that abuse was handed out by patients and their families, the bulk again came from their "bosses"—physicians.

Among the consequences of verbal abuse that Sofield and Salmond reported were decreased morale, experienced by 67 percent of those surveyed; decreased productivity, reported by 41 percent; and increased errors, reported by 51 percent. In addition, 13.6 percent of those surveyed said that they had left a nursing position because of verbal abuse incurred in the position, and 67 percent stated that verbal abuse contributes to the ongoing shortage of nurses.

50—WELL 10, ANYWAY—WAYS TO LEAVE YOUR BULLY (WITH APOLOGIES TO PAUL SIMON)

1. Just put on your hat, Jack.
2. Go for a run, son.
3. Tell him good-bye, Sly.
4. Pack up your desk, Bess.
5. Laugh in her face, Grace.
6. Stand up to her guff, Buff.
7. Say he's a pain, Jane.
8. Complain to his boss, Ross.
9. Tell him you're gone, John.
10. Get a new job, Bob.

Other professions are plagued by similar problems. In a 2001 survey of Australian workers conducted by human resources firm TMP Worldwide, 33 percent of those surveyed in the legal profession said they experienced regular bullying from their employer or manager. In the government sector, 22 percent of workers surveyed said their employers were bullies.

An October 2002 survey from Mercer Human Resource Consulting found that more than one in five British employees (21 percent) reported that they had been bullied at least once during the prior 23 months. The study found the highest incidence of bullying in the public heath-care sector, where nearly three in 10, or 28 percent, reported being bullied at least once in the last year.

Mercer also reported that 28 percent of the more than 3,500 British workers surveyed said that they had been bullied at least once in the preceding 12 months. The survey found that the sector least affected by bullying was retail, where less than 18 percent of workers said they have been bullied. But 18 percent, or nearly one out of five workers, is still a substantial number.

The research also reveals that eight percent of respondents said that they had been bullied on several occasions, while two percent reported that they had been bullied six or more times in the prior year. Extrapolated to the UK workforce, these findings indicate that more than 1.5 million workers could be the victims of repeated bullying at work, the authors of the study concluded.

The study also reported that 24 percent of middle managers and 17 percent of senior managers said they had been bullied at least once over the past year.

2.

PROFILE OF A BULLY

For many bullies, psychologists say, the abuse they deliver represents their distorted means of coping with their own problems of low self-esteem, a troubled childhood or dysfunctional family life. Their favorite targets are, not surprisingly, those whom they perceive as the most vulnerable, those who either choose not to or cannot stand up to the bully. And if those same individuals exhibit qualities that the bully covets, the result is a portrait of the perfect target.

Bullies, whether in the schoolyard or the office, undermine and frighten their victims in an effort to cope with their own fears, direct attention away from their shortcomings and aggrandize themselves. Moreover, they frequently choose those who have the skills to do the job better than they do.

Of course, in order to preserve their self-image, bullies seldom recognize the traits that make them what they are, mistaking their aggression for decisiveness, cruelty for candor, irrationality for flexibility and obsession with trivia for thoroughness. They will rarely, if ever, admit to being wrong. When a mistake is made, it is inevitably somebody else's fault.

Clinical psychologist Chris Nordgren noted in an interview that the abuser may not realize that he or she is abusive. Indeed, experts note, many bullying managers have some of the features of a personality disorder, while others may have full-blown personality disorders. However, not every bully has a personality disorder or experienced a troubled childhood; some are just plain mean. And regardless of what makes your bully a bully, well, that's his problem. It is not your burden to bear.

Some individuals may switch abruptly from being personable, even charming, to abusive, Nordgren adds. These characteristics fit

NARCISSISTIC PERSONALITY DISORDER

According to the *The Diagnostic and Statistical Manual of Mental Disorders, Fourth Edition (DSM-IV)* by the American Psychiatric Association, criteria for narcissistic personality disorder include a pervasive pattern of grandiosity, a need for admiration, and a lack of empathy, as indicated by five or more of the following:

· an exaggerated sense of self importance

· a preoccupation with fantasies of unlimited success, power, brilliance, beauty, or ideal love

· a belief that he or she is "special" and can only be understood by, or should associate with, other special or high-status people or entities

· a requirement of excessive admiration

· a feeling of a sense of entitlement, i.e., unreasonable expectations of especially favorable treatment or automatic compliance with his or her expectations

· a habit of being interpersonally exploitative, i.e., takes advantage of others to achieve his or her own ends

· a lack of empathy, i.e., is unwilling to recognize or identify with the feelings and needs of others

· an envy of others or a belief that others are envious of him or her

a borderline personality disorder. Such individuals may truly believe they are communicating effectively, but then are disappointed, perhaps enraged, when their expectations are not met.

Bullies' expectations may also change constantly, without warning, yet employees are still, somehow, required to recognize and meet those expectations. While bullies may be motivated by an array of needs, one that they, by definition, all share is the need to control others, whether by verbal abuse, physical actions or some combination of the two.

Typically lacking sympathy for the problems of others, bullies often do not even recognize that others have problems, so wrapped up are they in their own concerns. Often short-tempered and angry, they tend to impute to others the hostility and aggressiveness they themselves feel.

Whether female or male, they often have experienced physical/or and emotional abuse themselves. Their behavior is frequently characterized by obsessive or overly rigid actions, including incessant nit-picking and excessive focus on trivia, often magnifying, distorting, or misrepresenting the problems they perceive.

Although they may berate their victims for not being team players, bullying bosses seldom have any real sense of what constitutes teamwork. They tend to exaggerate their own contributions and are reluctant to acknowledge the contributions of others. They adopt a territorial approach to running their workplaces and often use loud, aggressive tactics to dominate decision making and day-to-day operations. Differing viewpoints are ignored, if not actually ridiculed. There is only one right way, the bully's, to do things. Employees who come up with original ideas or who are eager to try new approaches are often ridiculed and/or perceived as threats.

While bullies may use screaming and shouting as "management" tools, they typically rely heavily on slightly less overt behavior such as criticism, insults and sarcasm to intimidate and harass their employees. While in-person meetings and telephone conversations may be the vehicles of choice, voicemail, or even email can also be effective tools for the bully, since they effectively prevent you, the target, from responding in real time.

But that time delay, as irritating as it might be, can also give you time to cool down and consider your response carefully before replying. In addition, by using written memoranda or voicemail as his weapon of choice, your bully makes it that much easier to preserve his comments as evidence (See Chapter 5, "Your Options.").

The bully may also express a somewhat more subtle form of aggression through a variety of nonverbal means, including intonations, facial expressions and other nonverbal modes of communication. However expressed, the demeaning content is clear to the victim and often, too, to the victim's colleagues. Over time, as the abuse is delivered in a variety of forms and array of contexts, the bully's objectives are achieved.

Bullies of both sexes tend to need to have all their demands fulfilled, no matter how unreasonable. As mentioned earlier, they often display elements of personality disorders, particularly narcissism. As a consequence, they demand respect and consideration from others—frequently flying into a rage if they feel they are not getting their due—while treating their subordinates with contempt.

If the bully's efforts to undermine and dominate his target fail, one of two results is likely. The bully may turn his attention to the next victim on his list, perhaps swinging by for a second crack at his initial target at a later date. Or the bully may remain focused on the first victim, escalating the level of humiliation and harassment until the victim has no rational choice but to leave. Of course, once the target has left the scene, the bully isn't finished. He will begin again on someone new.

AULD LANG SYNE

I thought about forming an alumni club for all the people that my former boss forced out of my old company. Just the people who had held the same position as I did would fill a small room.

I went back and looked some of them up after I'd left. We all reacted differently to the bully. I used to cry. One of the guys used to go back to his office after encounters with The Boss, and throw things at the wall.

None of us stayed more than a year. One lasted only two weeks.

Small companies in which the head of the firm is also the bully can be the worst environments, if only because the bully is subject to fewer external controls. However, larger companies are not necessarily much better. Gary Namie's 2000 survey conducted by his Workplace Bullying & Trauma Institute concluded that where human resource departments play a role, they often support the bully by reacting negatively to the target (32 percent) or by doing nothing (51 percent), despite requests for help. It's important to remember that no matter how sympathetic human resources personnel may be, their job is to represent the employer's interests—not yours. Sadly, according to Namie's data, 82 percent of those who reported being bullied actually lost their jobs "simply because a bully came into their lives."

In short, bullies come in all shapes and sizes, as well as in all types of workplaces. If you find yourself being bullied, you need to assess your situation carefully. To what extent is the bully interfering with your job and, more broadly, your life and well-being? Can you cope with your bully's behavior? Is the job worth the cost of coping? What are your chances of modifying your bully's behavior? Of transferring to another manager?

Only you can decide how much you're willing to put up with; how much you're willing to sacrifice in exchange for the ephemeral goal of "job security" and the paycheck that accompanies it. Take a careful look at what you're dealing with, and then decide.

LUPI'S STORY: A BACKWARD GLANCE

I stumbled across a micro-cassette tape containing a recording of a five-minute voicemail left for me sometime last spring by my former supervisor. Out of curiosity, I listened to the recording again.

The voicemail was filled with the most awful vitriol and criticism. Voicemails had, in fact, become my boss's favorite form of harassment in the last few months I was on the job (it was not uncommon for him to leave 10 voicemails telling me all the things I had done "wrong"). He was almost always incorrect in his claims of incompetence on my part, but knowing that never made it any easier to deal with his barrage of complaints on a daily basis.

Toxic bosses tend to be both intelligent and controlling, using guilt and shame to manipulate their victims, and insisting on second-guessing their subordinates every step of the way. Any faint praise can be counted upon to be the prelude to criticism, as can any attempt by the employee to act independently of the bully's micromanaging.

Rather than encourage the employee to show enterprise and initiative, and welcome efforts to improve existing processes and procedures, the boss responds negatively to any initiatives designed to improve upon existing processes, criticizing the employee for deviating from established procedure, regardless of whether that deviation results in improved performance, productivity or profits.

Bullies tend to prey on employees who show signs of weakness, notes Columbia University professor of psychology Harvey Hornstein. Once these bosses uncover a person's Achille's heel, they attack with a vengeance and zoom in on the weakness to create embarrassment and humiliation.

Others bully employees to mask their own incompetence. Hornstein says attempts to reason with such managers will backfire, incurring their wrath and, sometimes "uncontrollable temper tantrums."

In his book, *Brutal Bosses and Their Prey*, Hornstein estimates that as many as 20 million Americans face workplace abuse on a daily basis.

While bullying may seem relatively harmless in comparison to physical violence, the effects on the victim can be devastating. The toll that verbal abuse takes runs the gamut from strained relations with friends and family, panic and anxiety attacks, severe depression, and, at the extreme end of the spectrum, to suicide and/or homicide. Indeed, *Violence at Work* lists bullying along with homicide, rape and robbery as the most severe traumas inflicted in the workplace.

Some bullies fear they'll become less valued if subordinates step into the limelight or receive recognition. These often extremely manipulative managers will go to great lengths to retain power—even stealing a subordinate's ideas and taking credit for them. While they may appear to be the subordinate's ally, Hornstein says, such managers may prove deadly to their subordinate's career aspirations within the organization.

Another class of abusive employer may demonstrate narcissistic tendencies. In such cases, the abuse may be somewhat calculated, perhaps cycling through the office, focusing first on one individual and then another. There's a certain subgroup of "antisocials" who are smooth, have good social skills, and are at the same time manipulative and calculating, Hornstein noted in a telephone interview.

In smaller companies, workplace abuse often reflects the inability of one or more of the founders to let go and delegate not only tasks, but responsibility, to others. Even though these individuals may recognize on an intellectual level that, if they want their companies to grow, they need to let others assume the responsibilities they've historically filled, they are somehow unable to do só. Thus, despite having gone to the time, trouble and expense of hiring professionals to assume some of those responsibilities, for reasons of ego or insecurity, they are unable to disentangle themselves, making life very difficult indeed for their subordinates.

Unfortunately, because of all the boss has invested in his company, the subordinate is likely to face a tough time communicating the problem, much less providing him with the information to correct that behavior.

Then there are people who have malignant personalities, what Hornstein, in a telephone interview, termed "low-grade sadists." These folks actually enjoy, and cannot do without, tormenting their subordinates. Often these individuals are superficially charming, and may appear perfectly reasonable in most situations.

That's the extreme, of course. But if that behavior is in place, it tends to filter down through the ranks, influencing the bully's subordinates to behave in similar ways to their subordinates. That, in turn, Hornstein says, sets up an adversarial "them versus us" mindset that permeates the entire company, rather than an environment in which all employees are viewed as part of a team with shared goals. It's not so much that bullies want to denigrate their subordinates, Hornstein notes. "Rather they want to elevate themselves. It's a natural human tendency." In bullies, however, that tendency may run amok, unchecked by the notion that the needs of one's subordinates are worthy of consideration.

While some bullies may be sadists, others may simply be unaware of or indifferent to the impact they are having on their subordinates, comments Ed Beck of the Susquehanna Institute in a telephone interview. "These individuals have lost all sense of appropriate boundaries, and let things get out of hand. They either lose it, or somehow think it will be tolerated." But harassment does not have to be tolerated. Very few of us, he notes, get paid enough to feel lousy.

Beck makes an important distinction between the manager's legitimate authority and the abuse of such authority. For example, if a manager criticizes a sales rep for not meeting previously stated, agreed-upon goals within a certain period of time, that's legitimate criticism, assuming it is made in a civil manner. But if the employee was never made aware of the manager's expectations, or if those expectations change from day to day, that's a different story. Unless the employee's job description includes the requirement that the employee somehow must anticipate the needs of the employer, criticizing the employee for not reading the manager's mind, at the minimum, verges on harassment.

In many cases, bullies are neither sadists nor oblivious to the impact they have on their subordinates. Many individuals simply believe in management by intimidation, to keep the staff guessing and on their toes. However, while such a tactic may seem effective in the shorter term, it is less so over the longer term, resulting in increased turnover, high absenteeism and reduced initiative (See Chapter 16, "The Not-So-Hidden Costs of Workplace Bullying.").

ELLEN'S STORY

I worked for smaller companies, and the bullies were always owners of the company. I worked for a series of companies spanning 10 years and about seven companies with the same pattern of abuse—small, privately owned publishing companies and ad agencies that sometimes employed family members, where hired help was subjected to rubber-band management, high levels of burnout, impossible deadlines and workload. Our only recourse was to quit. There was no such thing as human resources or any kind of due process. Raises were a joke.

To get a raise, you quit and found another job. There was no such thing as retirement, sick leave or vacation. Anyone who took a vacation for longer than three to four days was summarily fired upon return. The logic was, if everyone could cover your workload longer than four days, you were unnecessary. I started my own business to provide my own job to get away from it all. My health nearly failed completely under the stress.

Tim Field, well-known in the UK for his studies of verbal abuse and bullying in the workplace, put it this way in an email interview: "The serial bully seems to have the intelligence of an adult, but with the emotions of a five-year-old. Engaging in verbal dialogue with a serial bully is like trying to nail jelly to a tree. Nothing works. Normal methods of communications—conversation, adult-adult [dialogue], justification, explanation, appeasement, apology, mediation, conciliation, arbitration, negotiation—all fail. And the fact that nothing works drives the target up the wall."

FAILURE TO COMMUNICATE

Perhaps your manager has genuine concerns but is clumsy and/or unprofessional in his approach to management. Take a step back to make sure you're distinguishing between genuine feedback, even feedback undiplomatically presented, and bullying. Bullying typically:

- is persistent

- does not provide useful feedback

- focuses on trivial issues

- is based on false or distorted allegations

- relates to unrealistic or unreasonable targets that are set arbitrarily

- is not accompanied by constructive efforts to resolve the issue

As you review your manager's actions and behavior, consider whether your manager is in fact toxic, effectively poisoning your working environment through persistent abuse, whether subtle or overt, or whether he is simply a poor manager or an ineffective communicator. If the latter description fits, you may be dealing with someone who's essentially reasonable, but who lacks the appropriate skills, is inexperienced or is under pressure.

Very likely, you can work with such an individual to receive the information and feedback you need and perhaps even reverse roles—subtly of course—prompting him to improve his management, enabling you to do your work. An essentially reasonable manager can eventually respond constructively if you persist, politely, in your efforts to communicate. The good news is, while having to "manage your manager" is far from ideal, it's a big improvement over having to cope with a bullying boss.

STRENGTH IN NUMBNESS: THE ZEN OF DENIAL

Because bullying is often a relatively subtle and cumulative process, targets may not be fully aware of the impact their workplace is having on them until long after it has begun to take its toll. This phenomenon delays diagnosis, treatment, and recovery.

As the bully hones in on his target, the abuse slowly escalates in impact and intensity. Yet each incident, in isolation, could be considered minor. Frequently, neither targets nor their coworkers are aware until relatively late in the process that such behavior is in fact taking place. And one day, you, the employee, find yourself struggling to meet objectives that either can never be met or, when met, will change once again.

MIRIAM'S STORY

Although the group policy was to rotate proofreading among members because it is a tedious task, I had been the sole proofreader in the group for over two years—by decision of my manager. Sure enough, she found a typo I had missed and summoned me to her office. From now on, she said, she was only going to track my errors—not my accomplishments. She insisted that doing a good job was what I was paid for, and I need not receive any credit for that.

Effects on behavior and personality, including loss of self-confidence and self-image, are well addressed elsewhere. See for example, Tim Field's *Bully in Sight*, Gary and Ruth Namie's *The Bully at Work*, and Harvey's Hornstein's *Brutal Bosses and Their Prey*. Briefly, though, those effects may include bouts of crying, irritability, anger, indecision and withdrawal, just to name a few common consequences. If you find your behavior and/or mood take a turn for the worse, take some time out to assess what is happening and why.

Bullying bosses are extremely manipulative, exhibiting a constant need to be fully in control. Sometimes literally oblivious to those around them, they dictate how and what decisions are made, allowing no real debate.

As a consequence, you'd think they'd be easy to spot. Oddly, they often are not, at least not initially. Bullies frequently are chameleons, superficially charming, even ingratiating. But once they've focused in on a target—whether a subordinate or a peer—the charm abruptly vanishes, leaving the victim, who's finally realized just what he's got himself into, in a state of panic.

In addition to dismissing or minimizing the contributions of others, bullying managers exaggerate their own contributions to themselves and to others, and reject the possibility that anyone else might have an original contribution, a fresh idea or a worthwhile perspective. To a bully, employees expressing concerns about inappropriate or unethical behaviors or practices or proposing changes to improve products or productivity are likely no more than troublemakers with bad attitudes.

Some bullies scream and shout, others are a bit more subtle; criticism, insults, insinuation, and innuendo are their chosen weapons. Once started on a target, they can be inexorable and unforgiving, using all the tools at their disposal—emails, voicemails, casual encounters, company meetings, gestures, intonations, facial expressions, body language—whatever they can bring to bear to intimidate their target.

Some psychologists interpret bullying behavior as the bullies' means of dealing with their own past experiences of abuse and/or their lack of self esteem. Through their efforts to undermine and demean their victims, they make themselves feel powerful and in charge. And in their attempt to reassure themselves of their own superiority, they may turn on those who have the skills to do the job better than they do.

Once the bully finally hones in on his target, he is likely to be relentless. If he succeeds, the target is, ultimately, fully intimidated, perhaps to the point of physical illness, panic attacks and nervous breakdowns.

RECOGNIZE THE BULLY

It's always useful to know—well, let's not mince words here—your enemy. Make no mistake, how he turned into a bully is not your problem. You don't need to make excuses for him, rationalize his behavior or forgive him. But if you understand what makes him tick, you can work with that to protect yourself. Bullies often:

· use verbal threats and, sometimes, physical actions, in their efforts to control others

· anger more quickly, more frequently, and with less cause than others

· demonstrate little or no empathy for the victims

· exhibit aggressive behavior, particularly toward those who cannot effectively fight back

· wrongly impute hostile intentions where they do not exist

· exact revenge for real and perceived wrongs done to them

· lack flexibility in their actions

Once you understand the bully-victim dynamic, your next step is to decide how you will deal with it. That entails not only dealing with the bully, but ensuring your emotional and physical health as you do so.

WHO CARES?

If you have encountered verbal abuse and/or other sorts of bullying from your manager, you probably don't care—and there's no reason for you to do so—if your boss has borderline personality disorder, is a narcissist, is simply oblivious, or is just plain mean. The reasons underlying your bully's behavior are of utmost importance to him, his family and, let us hope, his therapist. They are irrelevant to you, if only because you have no power to change them.

Far more important is the impact that your boss' behavior has on you. Too often, by the time you realize that you're dealing with more than just a demanding manager, that trying harder or staying later isn't going to help, that there's more going on than a "personality conflict," you have a problem. At that point, your self-esteem has suffered, your anxiety level has risen, and you may be too emotionally distraught to take effective action.

Again, the first step toward regaining your perspective is

understanding that the problem is not you. It is your manager. Why your boss is a bully is not your problem. Don't let him convince you that it is. You don't need to sympathize with or try to help your manager. Your job is to get out. The genesis of your manager's behavior matters to you only because by understanding it you may be better able to deal with it.

Insights into what prompts your manager to be a bully may help you cope with the abuse he dishes out. By altering the way you react to him, you may in turn be able to deflect his harassment and otherwise modify his behavior (See Chapter 3, "Profile of a Target.").

But when you no longer want to play the game, the bottom line changes. Coping with the bully is no longer your challenge, no longer your priority. Instead, you will want to know how you can move on emotionally, financially and professionally. That's the focus of the rest this book.

3.

PROFILE OF A TARGET

You have the sinking feeling that the boss doesn't like your work. So you work harder, you stay later, you take on more responsibility. But whatever you do is somehow wrong. By the time you understand that it isn't you, but your manager—and that you're being bullied—and you bring the issue up with your boss, it's very likely too late.

At this point, attempts to resolve the problem may only produce painful encounters in which the bully hears just what he wants to hear, and can conclude the meeting feeling satisfied that he has fulfilled his function as a manager and perhaps even as a "coach." He might also glean additional material for your personnel file when your inability to communicate your side of the story escalates to frustration and possibly even tears. (We'll take a look at some possible strategies for dealing with this type of encounter later in this chapter.)

The meeting, from the employer's perspective, is a success. He has firmly drummed into you the degree to which your work does not meet his expectations, has stressed that those expectations must be met, and reiterated his view of your incompetence. And, last but not least, he has demonstrated to both you and to your coworkers the perils of opposing him.

From your point of view, the meeting is likely no more than the most recent in a series of disasters in which you are once again subjected to abuse and offered no fair opportunity for rebuttal.

You've probably been targeted by a bully if:

· your manager imposes arbitrary verbal and written warnings and procedures without justification, seemingly without reason, and they're directed primarily or solely at you

·   your positive contributions are not acknowledged fairly

·   initiative and independent thinking are vehemently discouraged and minor flaws or errors are magnified, never to be forgotten or forgiven

·   your manager bypasses you in giving direction to— or eliciting information from—your staff

·   you are required to produce more and more in the way of memos justifying your actions, while your level of autonomy seems to be declining

THE WRONG PLACE AT THE WRONG TIME

If you are the victim of verbal abuse and/or bullying in the workplace, there may be no more reason for it than that you happened to be in the wrong place at the wrong time. Sadly, and ironically, you're also likely to be the target of a bully if:

·   you are good at your job and thus possibly represent a threat to your manager

·   you establish good working relationships with peers and subordinates

·   you are older than most of the other employees and/or relatively expensive

·   you demonstrate initiative and independence of thought

·   you do not participate in office politics

Not surprisingly, bullies tend to focus on those over whom they have the greatest influence, paying relatively little attention to those whom they can't verbally batter.

Some psychologists believe that past trauma can make an individual particularly vulnerable to an abusive boss, prompting someone who has already undergone a traumatic experience to react to behaviors that others find easy to ignore. Other experts are skeptical, noting that most people have some sort of trauma in their lives. "The trauma caused by bullying at work most often eclipses all other traumas in a person's life," UK author and anti-bullying advo-cate Tim Field says. "Past traumas serve only defense lawyers who speciously exploit them to evade accountability for their client."[1]

Not all targets of abuse and bullying fall prey to their toxic bosses. There are some, who by virtue of their personality, their sup-port network, and/or other factors, are particularly well-equipped to deflect and even gain from their manager's toxic behavior.

Targets come in all shapes and sizes. Although they can be either male or female, studies indicate that the majority of targets are women. In contrast, bullies appear to be pretty much evenly divided between male and female. As mentioned earlier, not all targets of bullying are equally susceptible; some individuals possess personalities, defenses, or support systems that afford varying degrees of protection. Others have more trouble dealing with bul-lies, as the following stories reveal.

JACKIE'S STORY

I never, ever had so many problems getting along in a workplace before. With very few exceptions, I have always been a very well thought of coworker and model employee. I didn't understand that who I am did not matter in the workplace culture and the people I worked with.

They [managers] had me believing that they had the right to abuse me; that everything was my fault, that my feelings and my needs weren't important but everybody else's were; that I was mentally imbalanced, that I wasn't quite "good enough"; that if I just ignored or tolerated abusive behavior that it would stop; that if I just changed myself and had "more" or "less" of various attributes, took certain actions or inactions, or said or didn't say certain things or met un-meetable expectations that things would change.

However, Jackie notes, nothing ever did change, at least not for the better. The following are some examples of how targets of both sexes react to being bullied.

EILEEN'S STORY

As a participant in the highly charged, highly frenetic commodities trading market, Eileen is perhaps better equipped than most to deal with an employer who not only owned his company, but managed it personally.

I was brought there to provide stability, to build a company that he could take nationwide. But he was not the type of person who knew what structure was. And once he had it, he didn't like it. He confused people; his staff was often in tears. They didn't know what he wanted, much less how he wanted it implemented.

His ego was bigger than anything I've ever seen. He expected people with no commodities background to immediately know everything it had taken him years to learn. He wanted the company to move faster than its [lack of structure] permitted. He was holding people accountable for policies and procedures that weren't in place.

After Eileen came back from maternity leave, she decided she would no longer put up with her boss's irrational behavior, and filed a claim with the Equal Employment Opportunity Commission.

He was a raving idiot to begin with, and when he changed my compensation structure after I came back from pregnancy leave, I was actually very scared, but I was livid about what he did to our livelihood.

Eileen ultimately resigned her position, obtained a settlement from her former employer, and moved on to start a company of her own.

I'm a believer that if you work for a boss who plays games and runs with the hope that no one will challenge him, then hit him it where it hurts. I think that made him furious. Life's not fair, but don't be a doormat is my philosophy. We settled in my favor.

HALLYE'S STORY

Unlike Eileen, Hallye, a recent divorcée, was not as well-equipped emotionally and psychologically to take on her bullies. To make matters worse, again unlike Eileen, who had a claim under Title VII of the Civil Rights Act of 1964, Hallye was not protected under laws prohibiting discrimination. Here's how Hallye—who continues in a search for a new and better job—describes her experience at the hands of her employers.

I put all my efforts into work. I was working 70-hour weeks. I gave until there was nothing left to give. I remembered everyone's birthday and work anniversary date.

I did everything to try to make [senior management] happier. I worked harder and stayed longer hours. I put up with being ignored and treated rudely. I was lied to over and over again. And I continued to work harder to win their approval.

I wanted a way out, but felt I could not escape because I needed a paycheck and insurance. So I continued. I got more and more depressed. I would sit at my desk and cry. I prayed and prayed to God for a way out.

And one day He answered my prayers by giving me what I thought was a heart attack! Blessedly, after a second episode 10 days later and many tests, they only turned out to be severe anxiety attacks. I don't have another job yet. Still this was the best thing that could have happened to me. At the time, I didn't see that I had the power to leave, until I had no other option left but to stay there and die.

BRYAN'S STORY

Although women are the most common targets of bullying managers, men are also targets. Bryan has this story to tell.

I was hired as an admissions representative at a local private post-high school technical institute.... After a few days I began to have my suspicions about the integrity of the new director of admissions when I learned that the man I was replacing had previously been the director of admissions, was demoted to a sales rep and was going to find out when he returned from his two weeks vacation that he had been fired.

On several occasions, [the new director] stood outside my office door, and for reasons I still haven't figured out, made derogatory statements about me in a voice loud enough for all other reps to hear. Some of the newer reps were even afraid to talk to each other during work hours for fear of some sort of reprimand by this director.

About four weeks into my employment, I was called into the director's office. The director said that we needed to secure several more enrollees in the school very shortly and that if we didn't he was "going to break it off inside my ass." Just what he intended to break off inside my ass wasn't clear but it wasn't the kind of professional discussion I would have expected from someone in his position.

About six weeks into my employment we had freshman orientation, and I had more personal enrollees in attendance than any other single representative, by my count. About an hour after the orientation concluded the director called me into his office and told me he was terminating my employment because "everyone is over 'here,' and you are always over 'there' and it's just not working out." That's the only explanation I could get from this man.

Targets of bullying tend to be high-performing employees dedicated to their work. They often have records of superior achievement and have garnered high praise for their performance in the past. If, suddenly, their managers tell them that they can no longer do anything right and are constantly harried for their failures, chances are good that they are doing their usual more-than-competent work and have fallen prey to a bully. If their work at some point deteriorates after the bullying begins, it may reflect the psychological harm that has been done to them.

FOR SPOUSES, PARTNERS, FRIENDS, AND OTHERS

It's not uncommon for someone close to the victim of bullying to realize something is wrong before the victim herself does. Some common warning signs include:

- depression
- crying
- anxiety
- irritability
- nervousness
- shortened attention span
- ill health
- changes in sleeping, eating, and working patterns
- compulsive behavior, which may range from constantly cleaning to repeatedly seeking reassurance or avoiding certain situations
- forgetfulness
- lethargy
- clumsiness

· withdrawal from social situations

· excessive focus on work or coworkers

· fatigue

· fearful behavior, e.g., unwillingness to leave the house, interact with others, etc.

As a concerned friend or relative, you can help by pointing out, in a nonjudgmental way, these changes you see. Ask what's wrong and how you can help. Your concern leads to the single most important thing you can do: listen.

The best way to find out what kind of support the target needs may be simply to ask him. Does he need someone just to listen, to act as a sounding board, or does he want your active help in getting out? You need to maintain the delicate balance between providing support and pushing too hard. Here are some additional recommendations for friends and family:

· Encourage the victim to talk about what he is experiencing at work, and how he feels about it.

· Assist him in finding patterns to the abuse.

· Encourage him to start documenting his experience.

· Explore with him the options available.

· Suggest that he seek support from professionals, whether in the form of a mediator, a therapist, a doctor, or an attorney. Help identify likely resources.

· Read up on strategies for dealing with bullies and encourage him to do the same (See the appendix for additional resources.).

· Suggest, but don't demand, that he extricate himself from the workplace.

· Make it clear that he has your support, and that he is not alone.

· Remind him that he is a worthy, responsible, intelligent person, and the problem is with his bully, not with himself.

4.

THE IMPACT OF BULLYING

Bullying by one's employer may sound trivial, a rather mundane circumstance not to be confused with the truly traumatic events experienced by, for example, veterans of war or victims of violent crimes. Yet, bullying victims and victims of physical violence have more in common than is readily visible. Their symptoms, for example, range from heart palpitations, shaking, dizziness, and shortness of breath, to severe, even suicidal depression.

Being targeted by an abusive manager, or toxic boss, is more than simply an irritant; it can represent a significant health hazard. Studies done in Australia, Germany, Sweden, the UK, the US, and other nations indicate a high correlation between workplace bullying and depression, high levels of stress and a range of psychological, emotional, and physical disorders (See Chapter 16, "The Not-So-Hidden Costs of Workplace Bullying.").

According to a legislative measure that was introduced in the Oregon State Senate in 2003, between 16 percent and 21 percent of employees directly experience health-endangering workplace bullying, abuse, and harassment. This conduct, the authors of the legislative measure said, is four times more prevalent than sexual harassment. [1]

While the preponderance of working Americans will encounter workplace bullying at least once in their careers, bullying seems to become even more common in tough economic times. Not only does such an environment give employers negotiating leverage, but pressure for increased productivity fosters demands that leaner staffs handle heavier workloads. The added stress can prompt managers to vent their frustrations on subordinates, while workers, uncertain of their reception in a tight job market, are more apt to tolerate abuse.

But, regardless of the state of the economy, victims of workplace bullying are subject to ailments that range from the relatively pedestrian to the life threatening.

BULLYING AND PTSD

In a report published by the International Labour Organization (ILO), the authors summed up an array of research indicating that victims of severe bullying in the workplace are more likely to suffer from PTSD than victims involved in traumatic disasters. The author of the report suggested that victims' previous assumptions about the world and about themselves had been shattered.

Although pointing out that no precise relationship has been quantified between bullying and PTSD, the authors of the ILO report go on to note that the severity of the effects of bullying cannot be expressed more dramatically than in the claims that a considerable number of suicides may have their roots in workplace bullying. [2]

While conventional wisdom suggests that you can improve your morale in a toxic work environment by doing nice things for yourself—the "buy a new hat" school of therapy—such actions are, at most, a band-aid over the underlying problem. Instead, the best advice may simply be to leave, before your boss makes you sick.

True, the wheel of abuse may eventually turn and you may be off the hook for awhile. Even if the wheel does turn, however, is a workplace dominated by a bully one in which you can truly thrive?

If you do plan to remain for awhile, whether for weeks, months, or even longer, there are some strategies you can use to cope with your bully.

· Don't let the bully prompt you to question your own ability, and don't get sucked into playing the bully's game. You are contending with someone who is intent on dealing out psychological abuse.

· If you belong to a union, contact your representative immediately, but realize that your union rep may not be able to help you.

I REMEMBER IT WELL: RECOLLECTIONS OF A CONCERNED SPOUSE

It all came to a head in October, about the same time as the World Series. Her boss had taken to sending my wife Linda emails that contained such stirring lines as "We all make mistakes, but you've already made all that you're entitled to."

Frankly, I hadn't liked Pete from the start. Before he hired my wife, he would call at home to talk to her. When I answered the phone, Pete was rude and abrupt to me, rarely bothering with a "hello" or "goodbye," much less a "how are you." The job negotiations seemed to go on forever. It was mostly him, asking her to complete "trial assignments," and hemming and hawing while he continued to interview other candidates.

Linda wasn't thrilled about him, but liked the job as it had been laid out to her. She'd worked for a number of, let's say, idiosyncratic bosses, and had always managed to get along with them and do well. She thought she could deal with this relationship, too. I wasn't so sure, and really didn't think she should take the job. But it was Linda's decision. I was really kind of alarmed, though, when Pete made her an offer and it was below the low end of the range they had discussed. She eventually got it back up to something semi-respectable, but still....

When she started on the job, it seemed to go okay at first. Linda told me about times he exploded at others, but not yet at her. But then there was a mistake on her watch, a relatively significant one. She thinks she shared in the responsibility for it, but I disagreed, and still do. I mean, she had been there just a couple of weeks and was on the road when it happened. Vicky, the person who actually made the mistake, whom Pete had trained, had been there far longer, and the mistake made was integral to her work.

But, as Vicky's manager, and because she hadn't caught the error, Linda told Pete that she accepted responsibility for the mistake and would work to see it never happened again. That didn't help. He never forgave her for it, and never forgot about it. Pete would throw that "mistake" in her face any time something happened that he didn't like. At one point, he tried to "prove" that it was really her fault, interrogating each member of the staff, and asking them leading questions about what really happened. Another of Linda's co-workers told me this. As intimidated as they were by him, no one would say it was Linda's fault, but somehow that didn't help either.

But from there on out it was all downhill. His comments became increasingly strident and his criticism more frequent. He began changing her job description, adding new responsibilities and taking away her existing authority so that, as she put it, she had more to do, but no authority to get it done.

At first, she didn't seem to be too upset about it—she told me she thought she'd get over the "Mistake," as we had begun to think of it, and that her boss and she could move on from there, and work together. That never happened. He questioned everything she did, and assumed it was wrong unless she could prove that she was right. And then when she proved that she was right, he'd be furious, because, of course, he was now wrong. It really was a crazy situation.

Right about this time Linda became, well, emotionally disconnected from our relationship. All of her energy seemed to go into her work and, even more than that, into trying to maintain an uneasy balance with her boss.

I remember telling a friend that Pete was either intentionally driving her into a breakdown or forcing her to resign or both. I felt helpless. It's like you see somebody driving a car, full speed, into an intersection, and you can see they are going to run the red light, and there's nothing you can do to prevent it. You just hope to God that there isn't anybody in the intersection when they get there. I firmly believe that he knew exactly what was happening, and the whole time she was headed into disaster, he was pushing her to keep pressing the pedal to the floor.

She tried a number of times to discuss the problems with her boss, asking to meet with him to repair their broken-down communications, reset priorities, that kind of thing. But by November, he had essentially stopped talking to her and she to him. Instead, Pete would flood her with emails and voicemails. Most of the time, she seemed to be on the verge of tears, and she told me she was regularly crying at the office. And then, one day in December, I found her sobbing on the bathroom floor.

She started seeing a therapist who specialized in abusive relationships and started to realize that she was in something she couldn't fix. Soon after, to my huge relief, she made the decision to leave.

Diagnosed with post-traumatic stress disorder, she still has panic attacks, some of them pretty bad, and her self-confidence isn't where it should be. But she's come back from a very bad place, and is moving forward.

· Respond, but don't react reflexively to your bully's actions. The more disturbing they are, the more important it is that you take the time to cool down and measure your actions.

· Be aware that others in the organization may not share your view of the bully. Perhaps they have never seen his bullying side or are too intimidated to acknowledge the problem. Be wary of who you confide in.

· On the other hand, don't give into the common pitfall of becoming overly suspicious of everyone and everything. You do need someone—preferably away from work—with whom you can be completely candid and who can help by providing a reality check.

· Don't expect the bully or his supporters to be honest, either with you or with senior management and/or HR, especially if by doing so they're putting their careers at risk.

· Keep a record of the effect that the bullying has on your health, on your family life, and on the health of other family members.

· Resist the urge to retaliate. Not only will it mean descending to your bully's level, but it will undermine your credibility.

· Equally important, resist the urge to work longer and harder in a futile effort to placate your bully.

BULLYING AND YOUR HEALTH

Targets of bullying may experience symptoms ranging from shattered self-confidence to migraines to panic attacks to heart attacks. The physical symptoms vary depending on the target and the intensity and duration of the bullying. They include impairment of the immune system, increased susceptibility to flu, colds, coughs, shingles, muscle aches and pains, high blood pressure, skin problems, and irritable bowel syndrome, among others.

Psychiatrists and psychologists tell us that bullying also results in stress, anxiety, panic attacks, shortness of breath, chest pains, angina, dizziness, numbness, obsessive behaviors, inability to concentrate, insomnia, fatigue, depression, headaches, trembling, weight loss or gain, and hormonal problems.

Researchers also have found evidence that diabetes, asthma, allergies, fibromyalgia, multiple sclerosis, bone density loss, chronic fatigue syndrome, and some forms of cancer may be aggravated, or perhaps even caused, by stress and depression.

In short, the toll that being the target of bullying takes can be serious, even deadly. Constant high levels of stress and anxiety not only foster depression and anger (whether outwardly or inwardly directed), they can also result in physical symptoms. The prospect of going to work, any fleeting reminder of the bully or the sound of his approach can abruptly trigger those symptoms. And when endured or ignored, that stress response can become dangerous, sometimes lethal.

Victims ténd to internalize anger rather than express it, which sometimes results in major depression. Such individuals may harm themselves by using alcohol or drugs, or by attempting or committing suicide. Others may turn their anger outward, engaging in activities ranging from throwing things and yelling at family and friends to kicking the dog and driving overly aggressively.

There is no one reaction, but if you find yourself avoiding tasks that were formerly routine, engaging in long bouts of daydreaming, or thinking at all bout how bad you are at your job, you need to find a way to leave. And if you begin to think, even only "half-seriously," of suicide, waste no time in finding professional help. In this situation, the job could literally be killing you. For some small minority, not leaving the job could result in a reaction on the other end of the spectrum. The victim may turn his anger outward, returning to the workplace with violence in mind.

5.

YOUR OPTIONS

At some point along the way, many targets of workplace bullying, with their self-confidence and self-esteem undermined, cease to trust their judgment and start to doubt their instincts, reducing their capacity to make difficult decisions. At the same time, however, these individuals are faced with one of the most important decisions they will ever confront: how to deal with their toxic environment and bullying boss.

Stay or leave? Fight or get on with your life? Learn to tolerate the abuse or blow the whistle on a bully. The choice is yours. But before you decide, give careful consideration to the toll your choice will take on you and on your family. Make sure you're ready to deal with whatever you decide. Do you have the support you'll need to help you through whatever choice you make? If not, now is the time to put your "team" together. To recover from your experience, you will need resolution and closure. One of your first goals, perhaps with the help of a therapist, is to determine what resolution and closure involves for you.

The answer may or may not include litigation, which can take years to run its course, years during which you will not have the resolution you seek. You also need to keep in mind that, realistically, the outcome of litigation may not be in your favor. Current US law is less than friendly to targets of "equal opportunity" workplace abuse, that is, abuse not tied to forms of discrimination recognized by law. Thus, regardless of the experience you've undergone, your success is not assured. If, however, you can link your cases to one of the protected categories (such as gender, race or religion) defined under federal law (See Chapter 9, "Your Day in Court?".), your case is likely to be much stronger. Keep in mind however, that legal standards are always in flux, and often differ from jurisdiction to jurisdiction. Make sure you first have complete and up-to-date legal information from a qualified attorney in your state.

Perhaps you feel the need to expose your bully, so that he cannot harm other people the way you've been harmed. That's an admirable goal, which may or may not be achievable, and which must be balanced with your own well-being. Or you may feel that if you can just get your employer to understand what has happened, you will be vindicated and permitted to get on with your work. However if your manager is truly a bully, that is, sadly, probably not possible.

MARTHA'S STORY

I was subjected to workplace bullying and abuse for about three and half years with my former organization before I decided that I couldn't take it any longer. I had a breakdown while I was working for this bully and had to take time off work not long after I started. I was so spaced out I couldn't sign my name or make myself a sandwich. I couldn't remember how to turn the stove on. I was petrified of going outside my house. I had panic attacks when I was awake and nightmares when I eventually did sleep.

When I did go back to work—I made myself go—I shook so much I couldn't write down messages from clients. I had trouble remembering our policies and procedures and I had to rely on my friends in the office to fill in for me at the front counter when I burst into tears or had a panic attack.

Resolving your workplace problems is almost never a unilateral process. Unless your manager is willing to work with you to resolve the issues between you, chances are you're not going to get very far. And if that's the case, you need to come to grips with that reality. "Recovery started when I finally accepted that the working relationship had completely ended, and there was nothing I could do to bring it back," comments one target of workplace bullying.

It's hardly news that assessing your situation objectively can be very difficult to do, but finding the balance that suits your individual needs is essential. The lack of objectivity may be the reason that so many people stay on in hopeless relationships, whether professional or personal, long after they should have left. Unfortunately, by the time you realize your predicament, it's probably long past repairing.

At one end of the spectrum, job counselors may advise you to restrain any desire to tell off your employer, not to burn bridges, not to rock boats. No need to make your feelings known. Just get the best reference you can, and leave.

MAJOR IMPACTS OF BULLYING ON THE TARGET

· erratic emotions (tendency to angry outbursts, depression, crying jags)

· self-blame, guilt

· pressure to try even harder, work longer

· loss of self confidence

· insomnia, nightmares

· increased strain on personal relationships

· reduced productivity/efficiency, which prompts the bully to intensify his assault

· inability to enjoy life, relax

This is practical advice, except that many psychologists argue that, until you make your feelings known, you cannot begin to heal. They may recommend counseling or therapy of some sort to help put the experience behind you and move on to the next part of your life. Still, you'll want to choose your words carefully when speaking with a former or soon-to-be-former employer. If you are contemplating legal action, you'd probably be well advised to keep your comments to a noncommittal minimum. In addition, you may want to use discretion with regard to what you tell others, such as prospective employers, about your former boss (See Chapter 15, "The Second Time Around.").

Other factors that may play a part in your decision include the desire you may feel to expose your bully to senior management and, ideally, to dislodge him and/or protect others from what you've gone through. As laudable as these goals may be, don't let them get in the way of your health and well-being. Right now, that must come first.

Making the decision to leave even more difficult is that the abuse is typically a cumulative process, an accretion of many small incidents, each of which, when viewed singly and out of context, seems trivial. When you start to take them apart, you may wonder if, perhaps, you're overreacting. You're not. When you work for a bully, leaving is not a sign of failure, but a pivotal step in enabling you to regain control of your career and your life.

STAYING PUT

If, however, you are dealing with a bully at work and you decide, for whatever reason, that you're not ready to leave, there are some steps you can take to make staying on for awhile more tolerable.

· Focus your time and energy on developing a well thought-out exit strategy that will leave you in good shape, physically, emotionally and financially, to take your next steps (See Chapter 7, "Preparing Your Financial Resources.").

· Set limits for yourself and stick to them. Stop working overtime, don't take on extra tasks, don't work through lunch, don't beat yourself up if you make a mistake.

· If you decide to grit your teeth and endure your bully for awhile longer, make very sure you have someone, preferably more than one person, outside the company to listen to you, support you and, ultimately, to help you get out.

· Document everything remotely relevant that occurs in the workplace. Your paper trail can serve several purposes (more on this shortly).

· Don't lose sight of the unfortunate truth that ignoring the bully may be possible as a short-term gap measure, but it is not a solution for dealing with your toxic boss's venom.

CAN YOU COMMUNICATE WITH YOUR BULLY?

Well, you can try. Bullies, by definition, are not very good at listening. They are not interested in what their subordinates have to say, much less in what they are thinking or feeling. However, there are several good reasons for trying.

First, on the off chance you can get through to your bully, you may be able to persuade him that you're not an easy target, prompting him to move on.

Second, you're establishing a record of your efforts in dealing reasonably with him, which can help you later, should you decide to file a complaint or a lawsuit.

Third, and probably most practically, as you prepare to leave your job, you'll want to do so on the most advantageous terms possible. In order to do that, you may need to deal with your bully to get what you need. This tends to be particularly true in smaller companies. In larger ones, you may be dealing with the human resources department instead of or in addition to your bully.

While you may have given up on having—or have been intimidated out of trying to have—a rational conversation with your bully, consider trying it again as you get ready to go out the door. Even if he's succeeded in browbeating you in the past, you know you're leaving. You have nothing to lose by pushing him for a change into making a concession.

Depending on how your last days on the job play out, your options may vary. Whether you resign or are fired, your best chance for some type of severance package is if you have some leverage over your former employer—if you have a documented record of abusive behavior that is enough to take to court, or if your bully fears the publicity that your firing could generate. Ideally, you'll want to negotiate the terms of your departure before you leave. But if things turn sour quickly enough, you may need to salvage what you can after you've left, revisiting the scene of the crime armed with a detailed agenda and a fierce determination. Remember, however, that you have a choice. Chances are, you not only deserve, but can obtain some of the "parting gifts" you want. It's up to you to decide whether you're up to the process of obtaining them.

If you decide to go ahead, before you meet with your bully, write down what you would like to accomplish in your meeting. Include the details of the termination agreement you would like to walk away with (For more on termination agreements, see Chapter 10, "Getting Fired and Other Exits."). Then, outline the major points, give him a copy, and use your outline as an agenda for the meeting.

If at all possible, get a third party, perhaps an HR representative, in the room with you. If that's not feasible, you may want to check with your attorney about whether you can and should record the conversation with or without the bully's permission.

A WIDOW'S STORY

His only way out was suicide. He wrote to the Board, asking they stop the harassment. They ignored his letter. They just wanted to keep heaping on the power of the CEO whose shortcomings were reported, a report that was suppressed until after Chris's death.

There was no compassionate leave for him despite the fact that I was helpless with … a broken leg. He wasn't even given compassionate leave to take me to the hospital even though he was working seven days a week.

We consulted management experts who praised my husband's handling of the difficult situation in which he found himself. He was doing the right things by the textbook, but bullies don't play by the rules.

At the end, Chris was a very sick man. He was gray, emaciated, shuffling and broken physically and psychologically. The Board knew the bully's shortcomings and knew that whilst Chris was there, he would be a buffer [against] outright corruption getting the upper hand. The bully was sacked after Chris's death.

If your bully starts yelling, advise him politely that he doesn't need to raise his voice, you can hear him perfectly well. Tell him it would be to your mutual advantage to resolve the issues surrounding your departure amicably and swiftly. If he persists, and you don't want to or can't deal with him, walk out. You are leaving. There is less reason than ever to put up with abusive behavior. In any case, follow up with a memo recapping your meeting and your desired severance package. Copy your attorney, if you have one, his superior if he has one and/or the HR department, if there is one.

BACK IN THE USA

In the US, Ruth and Gary Namie's Campaign Against Workplace Bullying (CAWB) concluded in a 2000 study that:

·   twenty-one percent, or more than one-in-five US workers were bullied

·   eighty-one percent of bullies were the bosses of the targets

·   forty-one percent of bullied individuals were diagnosed with depression as a consequence of bullying

·   more than 80 percent of targets reported health effects such as severe anxiety, inability to concentrate, and sleeplessness as a consequence of bullying

·   thirty-one percent of female and 21 percent of male victims suffered from PTSD as a consequence of bullying

·   eighty-two percent of bullied individuals left their jobs (44 percent by involuntary departure, 38 percent by voluntary departure), also as a consequence of having been targeted by bullies

---

If the meeting continues, stick to the subject. If you want to talk about severance pay, and he wants to talk about something you did or didn't do, or launches a personal attack on you, remind him that a performance review at this juncture is no longer relevant. (Formality can be a great defensive tactic in a situation such as this. Not only does your frigid courtesy automatically distinguish you, for the better, from your abusive boss, it allows you to detach yourself slightly from the situation, enabling you to deal more effectively with it.) If he refuses to stick to the subject, or arbitrarily denies a request, such as the one for severance pay, point out to him that the subject has not been adequately addressed and let him know that you intend to follow up on it by whatever means are available to you.

Alternatively, if you don't feel you can deal with your bully in person, write him a detailed memo outlining your proposed severance agreement and request that he respond within the next few days (give him a specific date). Again, copy anyone appropriate, including your attorney and the HR department.

MAKING A COMPLAINT

Depending on your situation, as well as on the corporate climate, you may want to consider complaining to your boss's manager and/or to the human resources department. If you go this route, you'll probably begin by sending your manager a memo outlining your grievances, and sending a copy to the bully's manager or, if the manager is the bully, the company's CEO or human resources department. You'll want to make sure your account is comprehensive, detailed, dispassionate, and logical. Of course, this route is a dead end if your bully is the boss, and there is effectively no one you can send your memo to.

Assuming that you have an avenue of appeal, be sure to include a description of your previous efforts to resolve the problem. And, if you feel your argument would be more persuasive if you first tried one more time to communicate directly with your manager, one on one, do it. Though the chances of anything more than a major headache resulting from your meeting are slight, your efforts can serve to underscore your rationality and your good faith, and your manager's lack thereof.

Despite all of your efforts, an important word of caution is appropriate here: This strategy is as likely to fail as it is to succeed, particularly in situations where your manager either has the final word or his superiors and/or the HR department are not willing to deal with the issue. And, of course, keep in mind that your manager is not going to appreciate, to put it mildly, your audacity in complaining about him to a third party, particularly if that party is his superior.

DOCUMENTING YOUR CASE

Your best chance of success in winning your feud with your bully is to present a logical documented case that articulates, but deemphasizes, personal issues while zeroing in on business arguments. Mention the consequences of treatment being dealt out by your bully, such as loss of productivity, reduced morale and increased absenteeism. Emphasize that all these, of course, result in damage to the bottom line (See Chapter 16, "The Not-So-Hidden Costs of Workplace Bullying.").

One reason that presenting a documented case is an effective strategy is that it ensures that you're on record in case you decide later to sue or in case your manager makes false allegations about you. Documenting your experience may be important in the future if your job is ever placed in jeopardy by the bully, or if you end up in court. Moreover, as written complaints against your boss pile up, there's a greater chance that his boss and/or HR will be forced to take them seriously.

KATHY'S STORY

My boss is verbally abusive toward me—he is highly sarcastic and basically sneers whenever he talks to me. It's obvious to me and my co-workers that he is holding me to a higher standard than he holds my peers. But the more he wants me to accomplish, the less I am physically able to do. I mean, I try, but I can't focus. And it's getting worse.

I'm seeing a therapist, who has prescribed medication, but it's not helping. My husband doesn't understand why I'm making such a "big deal" out of this. He thinks I should just be able to shrug it off. I can't.

Finally, documenting helps you and others get a clearer picture of what you're experiencing, as well as whom you might be able to call on as witnesses and/or allies, and whom you'd be wise to avoid. Your documentation should take note of:

· Patterns of abuse. For example, do particularly bad episodes of bullying tend to occur on a particular day of the week? Maybe on Wednesday after the weekly staff meeting? Maybe after the manager has had lunch?

· The types, kinds, and frequency of abusive behaviors to which you have been subjected. What form does your bully's abuse take? Is he relatively subtle, interjecting nasty innuendos and sly sarcasm? Or is he blatant, yelling obscenities or ranting in your face? Or perhaps he swings from one bullying behavior to the next?

· The context in which the incidents take place, as well as how your colleagues react. Are they oblivious, or do they pretend to be? Are they sympathetic to you or supportive of your bully? Whom, besides you, is targeted by the bully? All of this can help you down the road should you choose to press a complaint.

· Your own reactions, behaviors, and patterns. Are you finding yourself hiding in your office? Jumping when the phone rings? Compulsively checking your email to see if something nasty has appeared? Do you find yourself starting to obsess on some aspect of your work? Do you find yourself becoming uncharacteristically depressed, tired, nervous, or lethargic? What is your most effective defense against the bully? Where are you most susceptible?

As soon as you recognize the danger signs, begin keeping a detailed journal, noting dates, times, and details of each incident, as well as witnesses. Include the outcome of this event, especially with regard to your ability to do your job effectively.

6.

SHOULD YOU STAY
OR SHOULD YOU GO?

Your therapist, not to mention well-intentioned friends, relatives, and coworkers may tell you that no job is worth the sacrifice of your mental, and sometimes physical, health. A compelling argument but, unfortunately, one that doesn't consider that you may have a mortgage to pay, children to feed, and/or other expenses to meet.

At the other end of the spectrum, equally well-meaning friends may advise you to simply ignore the bullying, let it roll off of you. Good advice, perhaps, but again, not always realistic. You may be in a situation where, although you may try, you cannot ignore it and the danger it may pose.

So, suppose you decide you can't afford to leave, but if you stay, you'll suffer emotional and, perhaps, physical damage. While your long-term goal remains separating yourself from your bully—whether that means quitting, transferring or scoring a promotion—you can develop and implement a short-term strategy that will let you survive this spot between a rock and hard place while developing the tools you need to extricate yourself.

MAKING THE DECISION TO STAY

Before you decide to stay and continue to work for a bullying boss, make sure you have a very good reason to do so. Don't let inertia or sagging self-confidence keep you in a toxic environment.

If you are staying at your job simply because you want to prove to the bully that you're not the inept, incompetent buffoon that he has made you out to be, then reconsider. You're not going to change his mind. Why continue to subject yourself to a bullying boss?

If you are staying in a toxic work environment because you need the paycheck and no other job is in sight—or perhaps you have another year or so to go before you can leave with your pension—then maybe it's worth sticking around for awhile longer.

If your decision is to stay, you then have two options. You can continue as you are and try to tough it out, or you can try to change your bully's behavior. Unless you can truly follow the advice of those who tell you to just let the abuse roll off of you like water off a duck's back (and if you could, you probably wouldn't be reading this book), that option is simply not a viable way to go. You need to change something.

Regardless of the route you choose, whether you plan to stay another week or another year, you should also be planning your exit strategy, both in terms of your finances and your career options. And whatever you do, make sure you have a solid source of psychological and emotional support to help you get through this period.

BEHAVIOR MODIFICATION

Face it, you're not going to fundamentally alter your manager's personality. For better or for worse, he is what he is, and it's likely he's not going to change. The best you can do is prompt him to modify his behavior. But even that is not easy and carries no guarantee of success.

You have two ways in which to proceed. First, you can try to change your bully's behavior by going over his head and persuading his boss and/or the human resources department to intervene and force a change. Second, you can change the way you react to his bullying, with the intention of thereby changing the way he responds to you.

Think of it this way: Your manager must be getting "positive" feedback of some sort from his interactions with you that encourage him to continue his obnoxious behavior. What's really going on? Understand the messages, verbal and otherwise, you receive from your manager. What response will he elicit from you? Will declining to provide him with that response dampen his enthusiasm for bullying you?

CONTROLLING THE DYNAMICS

A lot of the advice on dealing with a bullying or otherwise noxious boss suggests that the target systematically change his behavior, essentially altering his personality to placate his manager. Well, that's certainly one way of dealing with the problem.

But why should you change your whole life in order to try to please someone else, particularly when you're almost certainly doomed to eventual failure? And why, if it's your manager's behavior that is unacceptable and offensive, should you facilitate it?

Yes, while you are there, you will need to find mechanisms through which to deal with your boss. And that will mean modifying some of your behavior. But understand clearly what you are doing and why. And don't make appeasing your manager your life's work. Instead, by choosing not to react the way your manager expects you to, you can regain some control over your situation.

Direct confrontation will likely only make matters worse. But that doesn't mean you simply have to give up and cave in. Instead, keep calm. Stay professional. By not giving the bully the response he expects, you're destroying his rhythm. And, for a change, he's the one who'll have to react.

Train yourself to be able to maintain eye contact with your manager. It will make you look confident, and focusing on that will give you something to do with yourself while he is ranting.

In a similar vein, check out your body language. Just like your mother told you, stand up straight, lift your chin, and don't hunch. And try not to show that the bully has upset you. He may become bored with getting no reaction from you and leave you alone. Realistically, however, his growing bored is not a response you should count on, or even expect. He may not even notice or care about your reaction. For him, the bullying itself may be enough. But you will know that by refusing to cave in under his tirades, by declining to play by his rules, you're gaining strength.

Don't hop to his every command, but do address issues as promptly as possible. If your boss makes demands that are not reasonable, don't let them slide. For example, if the bully overloads you with work, let him know in writing that you cannot give proper attention to all of the assignments in front of you. Suggest a meeting with him to discuss setting priorities and re-delegating some of the work he's piled on you. Suggest a date and time, but indicate that you are flexible should he choose to propose another alternative.

If he responds by declaring that no meeting is necessary because you should have plenty of time to complete the assignment and, further, that you need to learn to prioritize on your own, write a final memo. This time say you are writing to acknowledge his response and will do your best to complete the project in an appropriate timeframe, but that you would still like the opportunity to discuss priorities and workload. Send him a copy of your memo, and save a copy, along with his response, in your thickening file.

Finally, work on the project when you can and go home at the standard quitting time. You're likely to find this surprisingly difficult to do, but do it anyway. Make a contract with yourself that you won't work overtime and keep to it.

If your boss complains that because you're leaving on time you're not getting your work done, acknowledge what he's saying. Then repeat your earlier request that the two of you sit down to discuss how better to set priorities and, if necessary, re-delegate responsibilities. Make sure he, you and the human resources department all end up with a written memo to this effect.

GET IT IN WRITING

If your boss provides incomplete, unclear, or sarcastic instructions, whether verbally or in writing, or tends to change his mind without bothering to tell you until the last minute, if at all, simplify and clarify what he says. Pin him down with a written memo of your own. If you're in a meeting, you might say something along the lines of, "I just want to make sure I understand correctly," and paraphrase what he has said. Get him to agree with your understanding if you can. In any case, send him a memo recapping the exchange and keep a copy for yourself.

A steady stream of memos may or may not slow him down, but it will create the paper trail you need. Whatever you do, you can expect him to continue to harass and bully you. Again, don't let the abuse just slide by. Instead, if your manager criticizes your performance, you might want to respond with something like, "So, what you're saying is that my performance isn't meeting your expectations. Would you clarify for me exactly where the problem lies so that I can address it and so that we can work together to find a solution?"

Again, he may never get back to you. If he comes back with specific points that are largely trivial, acknowledge each one. If you made a mistake in the past, admit it. Thank him for pointing out the error so you'll know to avoid repeating it. If no error exists, ask him again what the issue is. Be polite, but persistent. Don't let him get away with anything.

Ideally, he will respond, preferably in writing. Whatever he does, follow up with a written memo of your own restating what he has said and asking for clarification where needed. Your goal is to get him to reduce general complaints or vague directions into specifics. If he doesn't respond, or tells you to figure it out yourself, write that down as well.

If all of this sounds rather silly, that's because it is. These are steps that shouldn't be necessary among responsible, reasonable adults. But we're not talking about reasonable adults—we're talking about bullies. So putting everything in writing serves several real purposes. For one, it will place on the record any arbitrary or aberrant decisions that affect you and document your efforts to resolve the confusion. If your boss tends to change direction without mentioning it to you, and then blames you for not having read his mind, thorough documentation may curb this tendency and will help you should you ever need leverage in negotiating a termination agreement or decide to take legal action. You can be sure he'll have a file of his own.

If, at this point, you don't feel as if you have any choice but to try to meet your manager's demands, no matter how unreasonable, you really need to get out, if only temporarily, to regain some perspective. Do whatever you are able to do in terms of setting the kinds of limits described here, but don't push yourself beyond what you can bear. Instead, consider taking some time off, whether in the form of a paid vacation, some unused sick days, or even an unpaid leave, to help you regain your balance and decide how to proceed (See Chapter 10, "Getting Fired and Other Exits.").

If your boss goes ballistic, that's more than you need to take. Walk away from him if he starts ranting. Say that you need to go back to work, and leave. Then go back to your office and write down, in detail, what just took place. Similarly, if you do lose your temper or start to cry or react in any way that you really would prefer that he not see, then walk away.

Avoid one-on-one encounters with the bully. Whenever possible, have at least one other person in the room. This will serve several purposes. First, the knowledge that other people are witnessing his actions may tend to dampen the bully's enthusiasm. Second, one of those witnesses may later prove willing to stand with you if you file a complaint against your manager. Third, if the bully has fooled other people into thinking you, not he, is the problem, they will soon be disabused of that notion.

As mentioned earlier, courteously request (and keep requesting) that your manager provide or confirm all of his instructions in writing, and provide further clarification as needed. If he will not commit his instructions to writing, do it for him.

Do your job and do it well, but make a point of living your life. Don't be intimidated, don't get coerced into working late, or into taking on additional responsibilities without being compensated for them. Get on with your life and continue to document everything.

At some point along the way your manager is probably going to throw a tantrum. Depending on his personality, this may come in the form of yelling and screaming—at you and/or about you—or possibly he'll simply sulk. In the former instance, there's not much you can do other than to keep your attention firmly focused elsewhere. Yes, that's easier said than done, but the reality is that his behavior is beyond your control, and all you can do is document it. In the latter case, he'll likely intensify the volume of email, voicemails and written critiques. But look on the bright side, you won't have to deal with him face-to-face, and you'll have a written record.

In some instances, if your company is large enough, you can file a complaint internally. If you feel the bully is in any way violating the law—including discriminating against you or a coworker (See Chapter 10, "Getting Fired and Other Exits.")—then you also

have the option of filing a complaint with the appropriate government agency, such as the federal Equal Employment Opportunity
Commission or equivalent state agency.

If you choose this route, then the importance of documenting
your manager's bullying behavior cannot be over-emphasized. In
addition to keeping a detailed record of your interactions with
him, be on the lookout for witnesses to his bullying. When you find
them, ask them to affirm in writing that they have witnessed a relevant event (For more on this, see Chapter 5, "Your Options.").

Whether you take action against your bully or decide the
wisest course is simply to leave him in the dust, your primary
focus is to find your way out of a toxic environment and into a
healthy one. And, although by doing so, you'll be helping others
by reminding them that they too have options, your first priority
is yourself.

CODE PINK

Nurses occasionally use what is referred to as a "code pink."
When such a code is called—in response, perhaps to a doctor
furious with a nurse for not anticipating his need for a medical
chart—all available nurses come and stand silently around the
person being abused to lend support. Uniting in a similar way to
cope with an abusive manager and provide mutual support can be
an effective tactic.

The result is that the abuser generally gets the message and
backs down. Although the tactic is uncommon, those who use it
say it's very effective, according to researcher Laura Sofield.[1]
At the other end of the spectrum, the climate of fear created
can be so intense that employees may find it very difficult to
stand together.

Moreover, before employees can rally to the cause, and
often before they understand the full extent of the problem, the
manager has typically divided the group, focused on a victim,
and encouraged or intimidated others to join in isolating and
victimizing that individual. Abusive employers can often be
charming in a way that leads others into joining in with the victimization. Also, clients, employees in different offices, senior

management and others who do not have daily interpersonal contact with bullying managers may be totally oblivious to that aspect of their personalities.

Although allies within your office would be ideal, your best bet for support is outside of the job. But don't automatically expect friends and even family to understand what you're going through. Unless they're aware of what's actually going on, they very likely will assume it's just office politics as usual and tend to minimize it. Typical advice is usually along the lines of "Just ignore him," "Jobs are hard to find right now," and "It wouldn't be smart to give up your current job until you've found something new." To engage their support, you may first need to educate them.

If you are able to find a qualified therapist with experience in dealing with the targets of workplace abuse, he can be a tremendous help if you find you need to stay on the job. Make sure that the therapist you select is not only knowledgeable, but sympathetic, and firmly in your corner.

FINDING THE HELP YOU NEED

The following is an overview of some of the resources you may want to call upon as you get ready to make your move.

SUPPORT GROUPS

Internet-based groups are plentiful, and range from groups focused solely on bullying in the workplace to more general emotional abuse or workplace forums. Check out several and see where you feel comfortable and where you don't. Introduce yourself to the group, and see what kind of welcome you get.

Keep in mind that while many of these groups are an excellent resource for information and insights, their overall quality varies. Watch out for groups that have grown so insular and cliquish that they tend to ignore members who don't "fit," as well as for groups that are intent on promoting a particular agenda.

Continue looking until you find one whose members you respect and whose members respect you.

FRIENDS AND FAMILY

Don't assume that they'll understand—you may need to educate them. In addition to sitting down and talking to them about what's going on, give them the resources to help them see the bigger picture (See the bibliography for suggestions.).

DOCTORS AND THERAPISTS

Just having an MD or PhD after his name doesn't make him an expert on bullying in the workplace. Although, as discussed earlier, bullying is far from unknown in the medical professions.

If you turn to a therapist and/or physician for help, make sure that he's both familiar with the subject and sympathetic to you, capable of providing counsel as well as simply listening.

UNION REPRESENTATIVES

If you belong to a union, your local rep should be among your first stops. The willingness and ability of the union and its rep to be an advocate depends on the unions and individuals involved. But contacting your rep is definitely worth the effort.

EMPLOYMENT ASSISTANCE PROGRAMS

If your company offers you access to an employment assistance program (EAP), you may want to take advantage of that assistance, but first satisfy yourself that your confidentiality will be respected. Although most programs are required by law not to reveal information about you to a third party, there are some exceptions—for example, if you are deemed to be a danger to yourself or to another.

In addition, your records can be subpoenaed if you file a lawsuit claiming emotional damages. Moreover, some recent court rulings could have an adverse impact on the confidentiality of EAP programs. In 2003, for example, Dr. Sheila Horn was fired after refusing to reveal to her employer certain information about employee-patients that she believed was confidential. She sued for wrongful termination, but while a New York lower appellate court held in her favor, the New York Court of Appeals reversed that decision, based on the right of an at-will employer to terminate its employee. [2]

HUMAN RESOURCES DEPARTMENTS

In a company where the corporate culture frowns on bullying, the HR department may prove helpful to you. However, in all cases, HR works for the company. Your problem is not their first priority. If HR must choose between helping you resolve your problems with a bully and minimizing bad publicity, saving the company money, and following orders from senior management, it's going to do the latter.

LAWYERS

Litigation in the area of workplace bullying is very tricky. As in finding the right doctor, you'll want to be sure you find an attorney with the right experience, ideally one who focuses on employment law (See Chapter 9, "Your Day in Court?" for more information on choosing and working with an attorney.).

FINANCIAL PLANNERS

Would-be financial planners don't need degrees or licenses. All they really need is enough upfront cash for a box of business cards. So be careful. Take a close look at their track records. Ask them for the names of clients whom you can call for additional feedback. If they can't provide references, consider that failure a large red flag.

You can expect a certain level of expertise from individuals who have earned the designation of Certified Financial Planner (CFP^{TM}), but you'll still need to look further to make sure you're getting the kind and level of service you're seeking, as well as a financial planner with whom you feel comfortable.

THE NATURE OF THE BEAST

Can you really change your manager's attitude and/or perception? Probably not. His habits and behaviors have been long-since ingrained. Moreover, they've proven at least partially successful in giving him the attention and control he seeks. Unless there is pressure on him to change by those he respects or fears, your bully has little incentive to alter his behavior.

KAREN'S STORY: WORTH A TRY?

Whenever my manager-bully was in a conference with clients or in his office with the same, he would phone my desk and ask me to make tea and coffee, etc., for everyone. I didn't mind doing this as I quite enjoyed hostessing, etc. (my previous position was in the tourist industry, where I hostessed for hundreds of local and overseas visitors).

However, I did object to making beverages for the manager-bully himself. So I made a lovely cup of whatever for the guests and I made sure that the manager/bully's cup of whatever tasted like something from the sewer. Manager/bully never said anything to me about it but it didn't take long before he left me alone and started phoning someone else to make the teas and coffees for him.

Other times my manager/bully would tell me to type very thick annual reports (on short notice) for organizations that he was involved with outside the workplace that had nothing to do with me at all. I just let him put them in my tray and that's where I'd leave them. When he realized that I was "just too busy" to type them up in time they would disappear from my tray.

But assuming you or someone else is able to corner him and attempt to explain what's at issue, he likely will have no concept of what the problem is. Instead, he'll blame any problems on someone else.

What's really going on? The bully's behavior is simply the nature of the beast. Bullies are often incapable of listening well. That means it's up to you to understand the messages, verbal and otherwise, you receive from your manager and decide what to do about them. Statements such as the following, directed at senior-level people, ostensibly with considerable autonomy, are clear signals that the employee-manager relationship has gone south, and is unlikely to recover.

Statement: "I am open to feedback from you and will listen, but I am very unlikely to change my assessment of your work or my requirements for improvement."

What it really means: Not much interpretation required here. He's got the vocabulary "open to feedback" but no clue as to what it means. In other words, you can say whatever you want but it's not going to have any impact on him.

Statement to a senior manager: "Respond promptly to all my requests and seek my okay for delays. Follow all instructions to the letter and check your work carefully to verify that you have followed instructions completely before you submit your work. I will be extremely unhappy if you turn in work that is not fully responsive to what you are asked to do, is not prompt or is not proofed for completeness and accuracy."

What it really means: This is a relatively subtle act of bullying. In isolation, it seems relatively reasonable if the individual addressed is an entry-level employee with scant experience. It becomes significantly less reasonable when directed at someone who is essentially the manager's peer. Behind this statement is the implication that you're not intelligent enough to do the job.

Adding little gems like these to other run-ins with your bully will help to indicate a cumulative pattern of inappropriate behavior. If your company is of sufficient size and flexibility, you may want to seek a transfer where, with luck, you'll report to a less toxic manager. But not even that always works.

WHATEVER YOU DECIDE, DOCUMENT

Before you decide to take any action with regard to your employment, you probably will want to check with an attorney. If you decide to file a grievance with HR or to the individual to whom your bully reports, you'll want to prepare a carefully drafted memorandum formally notifying the company of your situation. If you are successful, that move may trigger a series of events that can extricate you from your bully while enabling you to stay at your job.

In addition to setting out your version of events, the memo should detail your successes on the job, summarize key conversations between you and your boss, highlight any inflammatory statements and mention any unfair or improper practices, says San Francisco attorney Steve Murphy.[3]

Don't feel shy about emphasizing your strengths and successes. Your bully will have no difficulty denigrating you, and anything you can do to balance the picture he presents—especially if backed by real results—can be a big help down the line.

By documenting your manager's activities, you are compelling your employer to investigate your allegations before taking any action against you. If the company that employs you skips this step and proceeds to dismiss you based on your supervisor's feedback, then it very likely is opening itself up to a wrongful termination lawsuit based on the claim that your discharge was in retaliation for the complaints you lodged against your supervisor.

Most states provide broad protections for "whistle blowers," Murphy says. That means that even if you ultimately cannot prove your allegations, if they are made in good faith, you can not be fired as a result of them. Employers who dismiss their employees for making such charges are leaving themselves vulnerable.[4]

If you're taking this route, you'd probably be wise to have an attorney involved, but only on a minimal level. Also at least at this stage, you'll probably want to have him keep a low profile. Lawyers tend to create an adversarial environment, which is probably not going to help you at this point.[5] In other words, think Joe Friday, rather than Perry Mason. While you're certainly making the best possible case for yourself, you want to make it dispassionately and logically.

Should your employer learn that you have consulted an attorney, the rules of the game will inevitably change, and the stakes become even higher as the employer brings in its own lawyer. At this stage, that's something you'll probably want to avoid.

As with other types of legal action, be wary of "whistle blowing-type" charges unless you feel confident that you have the evidence, the wherewithal and the fortitude to pursue them (For more on whistle blowing, see Chapter 9, "Your Day in Court?".).

Then, too, directly confronting your manager with allegations of lying, illegal conduct, or other improprieties will, not surprisingly, only prompt him to become increasingly defensive, and, regardless of whether they are legal, prompt him to look for additional reasons to fire you. So before you start down the road to litigation, make sure that you understand what you're getting into in terms of time and energy, as well as financial and emotional capital.

If you are contemplating legal action of any kind against your employer, you probably will want to review your personnel file—you have the right to do so, according to Section 1198.5 of the federal labor code. In addition, a related provision of the code entitles you to copies of any documents in your files that you have signed. You should seriously consider exercising both rights.

Your relationship with your manager may have deteriorated so far that the work environment already is unbearable. If that hasn't yet happened, it may soon begin. Submitting your memo could be the last straw for your manager, infuriating him so much that he turns your workplace into a living hell.

MEETING WITH MANAGEMENT AND/OR HUMAN RESOURCES

If you're taking your case to a higher authority, make sure you have reviewed all relevant documents, anticipated questions, and developed appropriate responses before talking to a third party. By reviewing your documents, you're preparing yourself for a rebuttal of whatever allegations may be made about you and, perhaps most important, establishing some leverage in negotiating your exit. Reviewing your records of what really happened is also valuable in fending off the false guilt that many bullying victims experience, such as the "What if it really was my fault?" syndrome (See Chapter 13, "Leaving Your Job.").

Despite the risk of failure, making the effort to change the dynamics of your situation—whether by subtly working to modify the bully's behavior, calling for third-party intervention, or filing a lawsuit can help you safeguard your mental health.

Studies of rape victims have consistently shown that women who do not fight back out of fear for their lives often end up more emotionally traumatized than those who do fight back. Similarly, workers who leave their jobs without making their feelings known or who suffer in silence as they attempt to hang on to their jobs, are likely be among the most severely damaged.

BEFORE YOU BEGIN

Your first step on your long paper trail is to identify your goal. Know what you want to document and why you want to document it. Are you considering, or have you decided to take legal action? If so, the nature of that action will help define what you need to do. Or you may plan to speak with your bully's manager and/or with HR, hoping that you can persuade one or both that you are not being treated properly and need help, perhaps in the form of a transfer. Expect your bully to minimize and distort your complaints. Here's where written proof and witnesses are invaluable.

Wherever possible, link your complaint to the company's employee handbook mission statement, press releases, or whatever other documentation you can find. If your bully shouted at you in public, called you names, used profanity, or labeled your work inadequate without providing an explanation, these may be violations of the company's promulgated policies.

However, most companies take steps to protect themselves from any litigation to which employee handbooks and other documents can expose them. Virtually all such materials contain disclaimers stating that nothing in its contents can be construed as a contract or otherwise negate the "at-will" employment relationship. At-will employment theoretically gives the employer the right to terminate employees for any reason, or for no reason at all. In addition, under this doctrine, employees may elect to quit their jobs at any time for any reason (See Chapter 9, "Your Day in Court?".).

Moreover, corporate policies often are stated in such vague terms that you may be hard pressed to actually define those terms. What does, for example, "a commitment to a professional environment" mean? And, assuming that you can pin down those amorphous terms, can you establish that your employer has, in fact, violated them?

MARCHING ALONG THE PAPER TRAIL

When obtaining written documentation, ask the bully to specify instructions, complaints, and punishments. If he will not, write him a dated memo setting out exactly what happened or what he's instructing you to do.

End your memo with a request asking for written clarification of any point you have reported erroneously. If the bully gives feedback only verbally, write that up the same way, asking the same questions. Keep documenting everything, regardless of how the bully reacts. By asking for clarification, you are making a constructive effort to resolve your workplace issues. At the same time, you are laying the foundation for legal action should that effort fail.

If you are a member of a union or a government employee, you will usually have the means to file a grievance. But keep in mind that while your union rep may be both conversant about your options and eager to take on your case, the converse may also be true. Particularly if your claim is not linked to discrimination related to a protected class, your union representative simply may not have the knowledge and resources to help you.

At any event, your representatives can supply you with the union's specific procedures on how to file a grievance. These will include timelines, details you must provide, and specific forms you will need to use. Be sure you follow the union's procedures exactly. And again be sure you have the evidence for the violation you allege clearly laid out in writing and, if possible, backed with witnesses. Don't waste your time, money, and energy if you don't have the proof.

WITNESS STATEMENTS

Gathering witness statements can be a tortuous and embarrassing process. You might even alienate some colleagues with whom you had—or thought you had—good relationships. But you need to do it. Witness statements can be key to a successful lawsuit or negotiation. Although you need to see if they are willing to back you up, don't expect a lot of support from your coworkers. Sad to say, few of them will be willing to express their true feelings for fear of facing the bully's wrath.

You'll want to talk to any of your colleagues who either have witnessed what happened to you or have suffered bullying personally. Ask them about the details of what they saw or experienced and, if necessary, remind them of what happened or what they told you previously. Be as thorough as you can.

Be sure to let them know that you plan to summarize your conversation with them in writing. If you have already hired an attorney, you'll want to give him a copy. Let each witness know that's your plan.

Then write a detailed account of your conversation, and review it with your witness. Make sure your colleague agrees that it is accurate and/or makes any needed changes so that it is as accurate as possible. Your next step is to ask your witness to sign the document, to indicate that he agrees that the statement is complete and fair. Give copies to both your witness and your attorney.

You will very likely find that your coworkers are reluctant to go on the record for you, for fear of losing their jobs or attracting the bully's attention to them. "I am convinced," said one victim of bullying, "that my coworkers would have lied under oath, had it come to that. Other than my closest colleague, none was willing to say they'd seen anything. My coworkers were a fairly fearless bunch, and savvy, but they were looking out for their own interests."[6]

If, when you ask your witnesses to review their statements, they refuse to sign or perhaps even to meet with you again, don't argue, but do try to confirm verbally that all of your information is correct. Then send them a copy of the final document in the mail with a cover note explaining that the document contains the information they had provided on the date or dates that they had provided it. Request that they let you know, in writing if possible, if they see anything that does not accurately reflect the events in question.

AN UPHILL BATTLE

Unfortunately, if you're setting out to convince senior management that your manager is a bully you may be facing an uphill battle. Bullies are often charming to their superiors and to people outside the organization. Very likely, they are adept at handling the people to whom they report, and equally adept at undermining their subordinates in an effort to make themselves look better.

If you haven't already witnessed it, you can expect your manager to take credit for successes and blame you or others for any failures. Because bullies are typically oblivious of the needs of the people they employ, they tend to push hard until those employees can no longer take the abuse. Thus, bullying bosses often achieve good financial results, if only in the short term. That means you'd do well to have sufficient evidence to persuade senior management that, for example, staff morale is low, which eventually will result in reduced productivity, increased turnover, higher costs for recruitment and training, etc., if it hasn't done so already.

By sending a carefully drafted memorandum to the appropri ate person at your company, you will put your employer on notice that you have a story to tell, and you may even succeed at opening a dialogue that will enable you to continue working there. Remember though that no matter how persuasive your evidence, how articulate your arguments, confronting your manager or seek- ing help from HR or your boss's superior may not succeed. Your bully may retaliate. He may intensify his harassment. Others in the company may or may not be helpful. You may not be able to take it any longer. Have a backup plan ready, ideally another job, in case your efforts fail.

THE VALUE OF FIGHTING BACK

Although your efforts may be rewarded with a transfer for one or both of you, sad to say, you're not likely to get a tangible positive result from your efforts to bring your bully to task. Still, the effort may nevertheless be well worth making. Despite the risk of failure, fighting back against your bully may actually help you to safeguard your mental health.

On the other hand, don't punish yourself if you cannot or choose not to fight back. Regardless of how you respond, the real- ity of what happened to you still remains.

RESIGN OR BE FIRED?

While some people argue that being terminated at least gives you the benefit of unemployment assistance, it also means that you relinquish control to your bully.

Although there are always exceptions, in most cases, it's better to leave on your own terms rather than being buffeted by the decisions of others. Of course, leaving on your own terms could include having your manager terminate your employment if you feel that scenario suits your needs, e.g., allowing you to collect unemployment or enabling you to file a suit for wrongful termination.

EMPLOYER TRAINING PROGRAMS

In hopes of preventing economic losses, some companies have developed training programs and comprehensive anti-harassment policies that include bullying. But these are relatively rare and their effectiveness is uncertain.

In a somewhat more practical vein, Section 5a of the federal Occupational Safety and Health Administration's regulations requires employers to provide "a safe and healthy workplace" for all employees. In theory, employers could be held liable in situations in which threats and other actions by an individual bully constitute a workplace hazard. But that's a tough case to make (For more, see Chapter 8, "Bullying and the Law.").

7.

PREPARING YOUR
FINANCIAL RESOURCES

Whether you've quit, have been let go, or are merely contemplating getting out while you can, don't wait any longer to put your financial house in order. In the best of times, organizing tax records and planning expenditures isn't anyone's idea of a good time. But it's got to be better than being served with an eviction notice. And should you suddenly find yourself unemployed, understanding your financial situation and having a plan to help get you through can dramatically ease your monetary problems as well as your emotional stress.

In the first part of this chapter, we'll look at some steps you can take to buffer yourself and your family from the financial pressures to which you may be subjected. In the latter half, we'll discuss some of the financial options available to you if you are unemployed as a consequence of a bullying manager.

BEFORE YOU LEAVE

If you can look at your financial situation while still at your job and realize that you have choices, you have gained control of the situation over your employer. "I have to leave because of my boss" becomes "I choose to leave." So, if you have the opportunity to prepare a financial strategy before you leave your job, use it. You will save yourself and your family a significant part of the worry that can accompany the loss of your job.

However, even if you and your job have already parted company, it's still not too late to marshal your resources. Very likely, one of the tools your bully used to manipulate you was your own insecurity, which he used against you at every opportunity. If so, then you may well have been persuaded that your talents are negligible, your skills not marketable, and that your ability to earn a living is minimal. All of these feelings make your being out of work seem much more desperate a situation than it actually is.

MARSHA'S STORY

Three times I've attempted to transfer back to my former department where I worked two years with great success and glowing references. However, that office's former supervisor has retired and was replaced by one of my current boss's cronies, who denied my transfer all three times without any reason, to the surprise and resentment of the department old-timers. That message was clear enough—the balance of power there has shifted, and there was no way back.

The truth is, you do have what it takes to find a new and a better job. This warrants repeating. It, in fact, is repeated throughout these pages because how you view yourself is key to whether losing your job is simply a momentary bump in the road to your next destination or a car crash waiting to happen. If, when you look in the mirror and see a bag lady or a homeless man, then you need to realize that your fears are not realistic. You need to find a way to fix your mirror and regain your perspective.

MAXIMIZING YOUR RESOURCES

Whether you've carefully planned your departure or simply walked out of the door one day after abruptly realizing you were fed up and couldn't take it any more, you'll want to quickly and thoroughly assess your financial position.

Of course if you're still in, or just coming out of an abusive work environment, the details of your 401(k) or the status of your health coverage have probably not been first among your concerns. In fact, if you're reading this book, there's a good chance that you are too worn down emotionally, psychologically, and physically to have been able to make the perfect strategic exit. However, you can still take control of your finances by reallocating your cash and investments to provide you with the income you need while adjusting your spending to meet your current situation. Don't wait any longer to do it.

FIRST THINGS FIRST

As a first step, take a look at what you need to know to make appropriate financial decisions. Understanding where you are will help you get where you want to be.

If you're still employed, but have a lot of debt, scant savings, little in the way of an investment portfolio, and especially if you are primarily responsible for your family's financial well being, you'll ideally want to stay on the job long enough to ensure that, once you leave, you have the resources you need to see you through.

Consider consulting a qualified financial planner to help you reallocate your resources. As with any professional with whom you decide to work, make sure that your choice is not only fully qualified, but sympathetic to your cause. Keep in mind, by the way, that while your tax accountant may be an expert in tax law, he is not necessarily equally knowledgeable about your investment options. Similarly, unless your financial planner is also a qualified tax professional and your finances are very basic, you'll probably want to get together with your accountant before tax time.

GETTING STARTED

Although being able to choose your timing and plan your departure enables you to take maximum advantage of the benefits for which you are eligible, that's not always possible. Nor is it desirable if it means risking your emotional and psychological health. However, if you are able to stay at work a little longer, you may be able to put into motion many of the strategies described below.

To rethink your investment and expenditures, you'll first need to gather complete financial information for all members of your family. This not only includes tax returns and bank and credit card

JESSICA'S STORY

Three stress breakdowns in one little office, and what has management done about it? I was angry then and I find I am still angry.

I worked for 20 years for a power company in a technical capacity. Our section had 15 staff members, many of whom had worked together for decades. We had much goodwill among workers and not very many layers of management. I was and am still proud of the company, which is extraordinarily efficient and usually tries to be humane.

But the company, like so many others, fell prey to the management mania. Efficiency! Seminars! Slogans! In spite of this nonsense, we took up the slack when new practices and software were imposed on us. Over several years, the pressure increased, with experienced staff retiring but not being replaced. When we asked about raises or promotions, we got laughter in response. We carried on for several years, becoming more cynical, and learning that management never meant what they said, no matter how pretty it sounded. Morale took a dive.

One day our section head and department head decided to hire a guy to do the front-end planning for our jobs. A great idea. But they did not hire one of the three or four sensible choices for this job.

They knew what they were getting. For 30 years, the new manager had worked for our company, and his management style had never varied: Trample and smear subordinates, suck up to superiors. He was a very loud man with an abrupt manner, and no people skills. Faced with complaints, his superiors would always excuse him, saying he had learned his behavior in the military. Two women who had worked for him in another department had taken a lateral move to my section just to avoid him.

Once hired, his original job description was abandoned. Instead of planning our projects to make our work easier, the new manager was put in charge of micro-managing us and doing our performance evaluations. He took over all liaison functions, breaking our ties to people in other departments, and telling them it was our fault when there were mistakes or late deliveries, painting us as stupid and lazy.

Disaster came within two years. For many months, we made frequent complaints to our superiors, ranging from fury to tears to cold detailing of the new manager's socially destructive behavior. These complaints were all ignored. Then, in the space of a few months, three staff

> members, one man and the two women, suffered stress breakdowns so severe that they are still under medication, almost three years later. One of them collapsed at my feet, in the office. When the ambulance arrived, I went with her to the hospital.
>
> I was the whistleblower. If I hadn't sent a letter detailing the breakdowns and abuse to several layers of management, the union and HR, I suppose nothing would have been done. Finally management took action, if you want to call it that. They hired a mediator to sort it out, and then on her recommendation, put the three on sick leave, forced them and the manager to retire, and gave me a small buyout package in return for my silence. They did nothing else, did not apologize, and gave the impression that it was just an unfortunate personality conflict.
>
> I have been out of the office two years, and I'm still angry. The men who heard all our complaints have been promoted. The corporation probably spent, in buyouts and lost time and mediator fees, several hundred thousand dollars on this "unfortunate personality conflict." The remaining staff, some still my friends, have lost any ambition or enthusiasm and are just marking time until retirement.

statements, but data on all of your expenses, whether for educational, medical or entertainment purposes. It also includes all your investments, sources of income and, of course, liabilities, which are your debts and anticipated expenses.

For the current tax year, gather up all of your receipts from doctor visits, prescriptions, and other costs incurred as a result of coping with your bully. Keep on collecting them. Prior to leaving your job, you very likely were unable to deduct your medical expenses since, if you itemized your deductions, you could claim medical expenses only if they exceeded 7.5 percent of your adjusted gross income. You might be able to eke out a bright side here, however. If you're facing a drop in income because you've lost your job, and if your doctor visits and/or prescription costs are high as a result of being bullied, reaching that 7.5 percent figure will become more realistic.

TIME TO PLAN

The more time you've got the easier it is to plan. Thus, depending on your circumstances, you may choose to put up with your boss for another few weeks, or possibly even months. For example, Tom Davison, MA, PhD, a CFP™ at Summit Financial Strategies, Inc., a fee-only wealth management firm in Columbus, Ohio, points out that if you have a vesting point coming up, it could very likely affect your retirement benefits, stock options, restricted stock, and possibly other benefits as well.[1] On the other hand, don't use financial uncertainty as a crutch to keep you at a toxic job. Your emotional and mental well-being are just as important as your financial health.

Whether you've already left work or are still hanging on, putting together a post-job budget is critical, notes Chris Long, a CFP™ at Long & Associates, LLC.[2] This information will help you to develop an accurate picture of your situation and get a handle on how much additional income you really need and the tradeoffs you're willing to make.

While leaving your job under adverse circumstances can be emotionally devastating, it does not need to be financially draining. This section is designed to assist you in gathering and evaluating the information you need to minimize the financial impact and move forward with your life.

ESTIMATED CURRENT MONTHLY LIVING EXPENSES

In order to understand what your financial position is, start by estimating your current monthly living expenses including adjusted quarterly expenses and/or semiannual expenses (e.g., car insurance and property taxes).

Put together a thorough inventory of all these expenses, including but not limited to, educational, medical, and entertainment for the past quarter or, better yet, the past two quarters. (As you complete this task, you can begin to review expenses and divide them into core and discretionary categories.)

Be sure to include expenses related to job hunting such as resume preparation, transportation, education or retraining, as well as those expenses related to the job you've just left, including legal and medical.

EXPENSES, ANTICIPATED OR OTHERWISE

Take a look at the other expenses you may incur in the coming months. Some expenses you can anticipate, whether it's some dental work for you, new contact lenses for your spouse, or new tires for the car. Some expenses you can absolutely count on, such as property taxes if you own a home and insurance if you have a car. Think through that list of inevitable expenses carefully and include them in your total. Those expenses among others will need to be paid. So, in order to take these into account, increase your total by at least 10 percent to help absorb unanticipated expenses.

ESTIMATED CURRENT MONTHLY INCOME FROM SOURCES

OTHER THAN SALARY

What income can you realistically count on for the coming months? Sources might include severance pay, unemployment benefits (which are taxable), funds from a cash emergency account, a working spouse's income, or temporary work.

List your savings accounts, money market funds, and other liquid assets. Indicate the total on each as well as income (i.e., interest payments or dividends derived from these assets). Make sure you know how long your employee benefits will last after your departure. For example, you might have a limited amount of time to exercise stock options. If you have any questions regarding the benefits to which you are entitled, call your employer's human resources or benefits department, and get the information you need.

CURRENT SAVINGS AND INVESTMENTS FROM

ALL OTHER SOURCES

List any stocks, bonds, mutual funds, collectibles, and other investments, including IRAs, 401(k) plans, annuities, pensions, stock options, and life insurance policies. Your most recent tax return has much of the information you'll need. So pull it out, and start from there.

SHORT-TERM STRATEGIES FOR MAXIMIZING CASH FLOW

THREE TO SIX MONTHS OF FUNDS AVAILABLE

If still employed:

> 1) pay off credit card debt
>
> 2) adjust your investment portfolio to maximize overall return without impairing your principal
>
> 3) use your remaining time on the job to maximize your savings
>
>> a) evaluate and possibly reallocate your assets
>>
>> b) assess your employee benefits and contributions
>>
>> c) use benefits that won't be available to you later— medical savings plans, employee sponsored health plans
>>
>> d) refinance or obtain a personal line of credit while you're still employed
>
> 4) look for ways to reduce expenditures

If no longer employed:

> 1) reassess your investment portfolio to maximize over-all return without impairing your principal
>
> 2) consolidate your debt
>
> 3) look for ways to reduce expenditures

ONE TO THREE MONTHS OF FUNDS AVAILABLE

If still employed:

> 1) adjust your investment portfolio to increase current income, maximize overall return without impairing your principal
>
> 2) use your remaining time on the job to maximize your savings

3) look for ways to reduce expenditures

If no longer employed:

1) reduce expenditures

2) consolidate your debt

3) examine your investment portfolio to determine what adjustments need to be made)

4) clean house: sell items you don't need

LESS THAN ONE MONTH OF FUNDS AVAILABLE

If still employed:

1) focus on reducing expenditures

2) consult a credit counselor for help in consolidating/reducing debt

3) examine your investment portfolio to maximize current income without impairing your principal

4) elean house: sell items you don't need

If no longer employed:

1) focus on reducing expenditures

2) consult a credit counselor for help in consolidating/reducing debt

3) examine your investment portfolio to maximize current income without impairing your principal

4) consider tapping "emergency" funds

5) clean house: sell items you don't need

IN ALL CASES

1) get a credit report on yourself as soon as possible and take care of any surprises before they can trip you up— ideally, you should check your credit report with each of

the three credit bureaus, Equifax, Trans Union, and Experian

2) review your last paycheck from your employer; make sure all the money due to you is paid, including payment for paid time off such as accrued vacation time, sick time, etc.

3) explore governmental credits and tax breaks

IN THE SHORT TERM

Now that you've tallied up your anticipated expenses and income, as well as your savings and investments, take a look at the difference between expenses and income. If income outpaces your expenses, then, relatively speaking, you're home free. If you've left your job, the more likely case is that you're in the red, with your expenses outpacing your income.

Ideally, you should have enough money in a highly liquid account or two (savings, checking, and/or money-market fund) to enable you to cover your expenses for at least three months. If you don't, we'll work on how to balance income and expenses a bit later.

In the meantime, though, whether you're in the black or seeing red, make sure your ready money is in an interest-bearing account that's earning you as much income as possible while staying safe and easily available. In other words, instead of a passbook savings account, investigate money-market funds and bank money-market accounts that are still highly liquid, low risk, and yield relatively better rates than conventional bank accounts. In a low-interest rate environment, the difference between a traditional checking account and a money-market fund may be negligible—in an environment where interests are high, the advantage of a money-market fund can be dramatic.

If, after subtracting your projected expenses from your anticipated income, you have money left over, then the next question to ask is whether you're keeping too great a percentage of your assets liquid, thus possibly cheating yourself of income you could be earning elsewhere.

If you have more than you need for the next three months in

highly liquid assets, like a checking account or money-market fund, you need to go to the next level and find the right balance between ease of access and flexibility on the one hand and, on the other, the higher returns you can achieve by putting your money in longer-term vehicles.

Move the cash you don't need in the next three months into high-quality short-term investments such as certificates of deposit and treasury bills, which typically yield slightly more than a money-market fund, but will still be available when you do need them. If you have room to move after that—that is, if that sum represents more than the income you've estimated you'll need for another three months, you'll want to consider a longer-term investment—see "Investment Strategies."

REVIEW YOUR PRIORITIES AND REDUCE YOUR DEBT

If, after assessing your liquid assets, your expenses still outstrip your income, your next step is to reduce your debt. Review your expenses and see how you can curtail them without radically altering your lifestyle. Dramatic changes may still be needed, but there's a good chance they will not be necessary. So take it one step at a time.

Think about expenses you can reduce: gadgets you don't really need, little extras you can do without. At this stage of planning, you're really just using your common sense. List your expenses in order of priority: mortgage or rent, groceries, utilities, car payments or transportation, insurance premiums, clothing, etc., down to the least important discretionary items. You'll probably find that a lot of items toward the bottom of your list can be completely eliminated, substantially reduced, or at least deferred. Here are some simple actions you can take:

· Discuss with family members how the job loss will affect family spending. Ask them for budgeting suggestions.

· If you're worried about your children's college plans, see what grants, scholarships, and low-cost loans are now available that might not have been when you were in a higher income bracket.

· Leave your Individual Retirement Account (IRA) intact, but temporarily stop your contributions to it.

· Minimize credit card use.

· Work with creditors and/or a credit counseling service to reduce or defer payments temporarily, extend the payment period, or refinance.

· If you don't already have a home equity line of credit, consider obtaining one for emergencies. As with refinancing your home, you'll fare better in obtaining a home equity loan if you get the ball rolling before you leave your job. However, in some cases, you still may be able to obtain such a loan, although likely at a somewhat less favorable rate. See the section "Your Home as a Source of Income."

· Sell collateral such as a car or boat to pay off the loan, but be sure that selling it pays off the debt you owe on the asset.

· Consolidate debt carefully. Don't transfer lower-interest debt to a higher-interest consolidation loan. Be sure your consolidated payments are less than your current payments over the same time period. And make sure that the new interest rate you're paying is not an "introductory" rate that will jump up to market levels or above once the honeymoon period is over.

· Save filing for bankruptcy as a last resort. Chances are you will not need to take so dramatic a step, one that will have a long-term impact on your credit and can add to the other emotional strains you face.

· Keep in mind that you may be able to temporarily reduce or eliminate some expenses, such as childcare and transportation.

· Clean house. Anything you don't want, sell or donate to charity. If you've worked for most of the year, the tax write-off you'll receive could help your financial situation. As always, don't forget to maintain complete and accurate records.

SAVING ON PRESCRIPTION DRUGS

An estimated 10 percent of US consumers delay filling prescriptions or are unable to purchase them because of the cost. That figure rises to 25 percent of those without insurance. Here are some tips that may help make prescription drugs more affordable in a situation where you are planning to leave or have already left your job.

SHOP AROUND

Prices vary among pharmacies, so it can pay to comparison shop. However, use caution if you get your prescriptions filled at multiple pharmacies. None will have a complete record of all the medications you or other family members are taking, making it harder to spot potentially dangerous drug interactions. If that's a concern, you might want to find a bargain and then see if your regular pharmacy will match the price. Many will.

GENERIC DRUGS

On average, generic drugs are 30 percent cheaper than their brand-name counterparts. Many doctors routinely write prescriptions that permit generic substitutions, and, increasingly, many insurers will only cover generic drugs. Check with your doctor, however, before substituting a generic drug for its brand-name counterpart.

SAMPLES

Your doctor may be able to provide you with free samples of medication, at least for a short time. Often, samples are also available for newer drugs and for drugs used to manage chronic conditions. However, if you'll eventually need to purchase the medication, check to see whether a generic version is available—using the generic version can save you a considerable amount.

MAIL-ORDER OR ONLINE PHARMACIES

Mail-order and online pharmacies can offer convenience, privacy, and savings. Although they can't fill a prescription as quickly as your local pharmacist, if you know you'll be needing a prescription and can fill it in advance, mail-order and online pharmacies can be a convenient and less-expensive option.

YOUR PERSONNEL FILE

As mentioned earlier, you have a right to examine documents placed in your personnel file. If you suspect that some of those documents may be libelous, don't hesitate to pursue examining them. However, if the statements are statements of opinion, rather than false statements of fact, they, by definition, are not libelous.

Statements that would tend to support a claim of libel include false accusations of criminal conduct, lack of integrity, dishonesty, incompetence, or immoral behavior. Thus, a false allegation of illegal substance abuse would be libelous if it were stated as a statement of fact and not merely as an unfounded personal opinion.

Be aware that a defamatory statement in your personnel file defames for as long as the statement exists in your file. Thus, memoranda placed in your personnel file 10 months ago or 10 years ago may be legal fodder for a lawsuit as long as they are part of your file. Remember, too, that you have a right to know what your personnel file says about you. However, proving you've been libeled is not an easy task (For more on libel and other forms of defamation, see Chapter 8, "Bullying and the Law.").

DRUG COMPANY ASSISTANCE PROGRAMS

A number of pharmaceutical companies provide limited supplies of free or discounted medications to individuals who meet certain financial criteria. Applying for these programs can sometimes be complicated, and each company has its own set of rules and requirements. Most of the programs require some income information, and may require you to document your income. For more information, check with your doctor, or visit the Pharmaceutical Research and Manufacturers of America (PhRMA) Web site at www.helpingpatients.org.

CANADIAN AND OTHER FOREIGN PHARMACIES

Consumers in the US are increasingly purchasing drugs from Canada and other countries at prices significantly lower than in the US. Although the Food and Drug Administration (FDA) says it cannot guarantee the purity of these drugs, Canadian pharmacies maintain that the drugs sold in the United States and the items ordered online from Canada are identical. You decide.

You should be aware that, in many cases, the medication you receive may be packaged slightly differently and even may have a different name. If so, you may want to investigate. Often you'll find you're receiving a formulation identical to the one you would receive at your local drugstore and that the drug has simply been marketed and packaged for a foreign market.

YOUR DOCTOR

If you are having difficulty paying for high-priced prescriptions, check with your doctor and pharmacist to see if they can provide any other options or resources that will make your prescriptions more affordable.

PREVENTION

You've heard it before, make exercise and good nutrition a priority in order to avoid the costs of treatment altogether.

MANAGING YOUR CREDIT CARDS

You probably won't be able to negotiate a reduced payment schedule for your credit card—although it's certainly worth a try—so be sure to pay at least the minimum due on every statement and mail your payment in on time. Keep in mind, though, that by making only minimum payments, you're not doing yourself any favors—your credit card debt is going to continue to increase and you won't even have the satisfaction of having bought anything.

Again, check into consolidating your credit card debt into a single, lower interest rate loan. While you're looking at consolidating your debt payments, check to make sure you're not paying an annual credit card fee—or, even worse, an inactivity fee for not using your credit card. There's no reason to pay either. If you are paying either fee, switch to another card. And, of course, make sure to cancel the first one so you won't continue to be charged for it. The following is a list of other small things you can do to get your finances in order:

· If you dine out frequently, consider cutting back.

· Avoid impulse shopping. You'll spend less if you have a shopping list that you stick to. You can save hundreds of dollars a year by comparing prices on shelf labels. Stock up on those items with low per-unit costs.

· If you're paying private mortgage insurance (PMI) and your mortgage is no more than 80 percent of the value of your home, talk to your lender, and see if you can cancel it. Depending on the size of your mortgage, ending PMI payments could save hundreds, or even thousands, of dollars each year.

· Review telephone, cable TV, Internet, and other service providers and look for less expensive options. Consider cutting back on home entertainment costs and reducing your telephone expenses by moderating your calls, perhaps choosing either a cellular phone or a landline rather than both.

· Consider using money sitting in a bank account to repay high-priced credit card debt, ensuring that your credit is good and that the cards are available to you should you need them in an emergency.

· Cancel extraneous subscriptions to newspapers, magazines, video clubs, etc. This may be a good time to dust off that old library card.

· Consider canceling memberships you don't use, or moving from a high-priced option to a less expensive one. For instance, you'll probably want to maintain a gym membership (regular exercise will help you stay in good mental and emotional shape), but do you really need to belong to one that offers valet service or other unnecessary luxuries?

· Conserve energy. You've heard it all before. Turn off lights in rooms that no one is using, set the thermostat so it's not cooling or heating your home when no one is home, and find a reasonable temperature for those times and for when you go to bed.

· Cut down on driving. Especially these days, your tab for gas prices and parking garages (not to mention wear and tear on your car) can add up quickly. When possible, carpool or take public or alternate means of transportation. You might also consider selling an unnecessary car. All of this should also reduce your auto insurance premiums. Check with your insurance carrier.

· Insurance is important, but make sure you're not overinsured. For instance, you might not care as much about a dent in your now 10-year-old car as you did when it was new. If that's the case, you can switch to a higher deductible and still obtain appropriate coverage for yourself and your car.

· Make sure you know what expenses are being automatically debited from your bank account or charged to your credit card. You may find some expenses that seemed negligible while you were getting that paycheck, but that appear considerably less palatable now.

· Prioritize your expenses and avoid late charges. Make sure you are up to date on key debt payments, such as your mortgage and car loans, or loans on other property that can be repossessed if you fail to meet your obligations. If you think you'll have trouble making payments, talk to your creditors and/or to a reputable credit counselor and try to work out a more manageable agreement with them. Some housing and car lenders, for instance, may be willing to negotiate a skipped payment or reduced monthly payments for a fee. But, remember, you will owe the difference eventually, so be careful what you agree to.

And the list goes on. These may sound like small sums, but when you save $50 by renting a video instead of taking the family to the movies, $80 a month by doing your own gardening, $50 a month by cutting back on long-distance phone charges, and $75 a month by making your own cafe latte rather than buying it at Starbucks, the savings add up quickly.

YOUR HOME AS A SOURCE OF SAVINGS

If you own your home, and are able to refinance your mortgage at a lower rate and, perhaps, for a longer term, your monthly payments will drop. If you're considering refinancing, however, make sure the process is in motion before you leave your job. Most lenders will not be willing to refinance your mortgage unless you can show that you and/or your spouse are earning what they consider a sufficient monthly income. And if they do agree to refinance your current mortgage, it will probably be on less favorable terms than you would receive if you were still employed.

When you refinance, you may wish to consider switching over to an interest-only loan with the knowledge that once your financial situation improves, you'll want to resume payments on the principal amount as well. With an interest-only loan, you won't be paying down your mortgage loan and thereby building equity in your home, but neither will you be stretching as far to make your monthly payments.

Don't get carried away, however, and get trapped in a loan that entails negative amortization. In such loans, your monthly payments are not large enough to pay all the interest due on the loan. Because you are actually paying the lender less than you owe, that unpaid interest gets folded back into your loan. That "feature" can quickly add substantially to your debt as you find yourself holding a bigger mortgage than you started out with.

HAVING ADEQUATE INSURANCE

If you and your family are active and healthy, insurance may seem like an unnecessary expense. But if you find yourself facing a major medical emergency without insurance, you could wind up being virtually wiped out financially and/or receiving a lower standard of care than you need.

If you are negotiating a termination agreement with your employer, continuing your company-paid health benefits should be a priority. In addition, try to time your departure to maximize your coverage. For example, if you left on August 30, your coverage would probably end on the first of the following month—September. But if you left on September 1, your coverage wouldn't end until the first of the month following that—October.

Once your group coverage ends, unless you can join your spouse or partner's plan, you'll have to pay the premiums yourself. It may be well worth the cost, which may not be as high as you think (See Chapter 12, "Protecting Your Health," for more information.).

Michael Dubis, CFP^{TM} and president of Touchstone Financial, advises you to look closely at all aspects of your employee benefits coverage, health, and long-term care, especially if you're close to retirement. Investigate conversion options for any term life policy obtained through your employer, he advises. "Life insurance you've purchased yourself may actually be less expensive—and will certainly be more portable—than that purchased through an employer."[3]

HELP FROM A QUALIFIED FINANCIAL PLANNER

If you haven't actively tracked your financial status and investments up to this point, you have enough to think about without tackling an extensive financial overhaul on your own.

But that doesn't mean you should ignore your finances. Find a qualified, and preferably fee-based, financial planner to help you assess, reallocate, and optimize your holdings to best serve your current needs. Consider it an investment.

No special credentials are required to call oneself a financial planner. Nor are financial planners regulated by state or federal law. As a consequence, you should exercise care in choosing someone to entrust with your financial planning.

Before you settle on someone, check with friends, relatives, and colleagues for referrals. Carefully consider the education and professional background of prospective planners. Check into their track records and talk to some of their current clients before making your selection. Financial planners who hold the designations Registered Financial Consultant (RFC), CFP^{TM}, or Chartered Financial Consultant (ChFC), or who are members of the National Association of Personal Financial Advisors have made a commitment to uphold codes on ethics, honesty and conflicts of interests.

Find out how your prospective planner keeps current on financial issues—whether through professional associations, trade journals, continuing education classes, and other sources of information. And, of course, find out how he or she expects to be compensated including fees, commissions, or a combination of the two. Get written estimates of the cost for services, and beware of planners who offer few or no investment options—they may have a hidden agenda in mind.

Expert advice is typically not cheap, but it may be a good investment. There are tax-wise ways of getting money out of your investment portfolio. Instead of raiding your pension plan and paying both taxes and a penalty, you might be far better off selling that tech stock you bought when things were hot and taking a tax loss. It may be worth your while to get your cash out and take a tax deduction.

REALLOCATING YOUR INVESTMENTS

This is neither the time nor the place to start exploring the intricacies of and opportunities in the financial markets. However, if you are invested in any combination of stocks, bonds, and mutual funds, it is time to take a close look at your investments and see if they're where they should be. If the closest you come to an investment portfolio is your wallet, it's definitely worth examining the financial options available to you. Your goal is to reallocate your cash and investments to provide the cash flow you need while ensuring that the balance of your assets are optimized for safety, income, and the degree of liquidity that you require.

Up to now, you've focused on maximizing your cash flow over the short term. But, ideally, you will want to invest a part of your total financial assets in a diversified, long-term portfolio so that a percentage of your portfolio will keep on growing for you. How you allocate those funds among investment vehicles such as stocks, bonds, mutual funds, and real estate investment trusts depends on your personal tolerance for risk as well as your specific situation.

If you have been an aggressive stock investor, perhaps focusing on one sector of the market and/or investing on margin (borrowing money against your account), it's probably time to take a considerably more defensive stance.

The more you are able to diversify your portfolio, the more "risk tolerant" you become. One concept that's useful, although not particularly easy to understand, is that, even in a conservative portfolio, your goal is not necessarily to maximize the income you receive, but to optimize your total return.

That is, you want more than just income—regular payments made to you, for example, interest earned on bond or money-market investments, or distributions of stock dividends. Income is just a component of the total return you're looking for on your investment. Total return is the overall change in the dollar value of an investment, over some period of time. So, in addition to distributions made to investors (interest and dividends), total return includes changes in the price of the investment asset (appreciation or depreciation).

By developing a long-term investment portfolio as well as a safe source of cash flow, you are creating a total return strategy that will allow you to benefit from price appreciation as well as from interest and dividend income.

At the same time, you need to think strategically about your investment portfolio. For example, following the axiom "buy low and sell high" may sometimes be a mistake. There are times when it may be advantageous to sell at a loss, getting the cash you need out while using the loss to offset taxable income on your next return. If, on the other hand, you take a profit from the sale of that stock, you'll end up paying taxes on your profit at the end of the year. If you've left your job near the end of the tax year, and so have received most of your annual compensation, you could be facing a substantial bill. Consult with a certified investment advisor to see which strategy is best for you.

YOUR RETIREMENT FUNDS

While the loss of your job is temporary, your eventual retirement may last far longer. With that in mind, unless you've exhausted all reasonable options, avoid withdrawing tax-deferred retirement funds to pay for today's bills.

JULIA'S STORY

Julia is a CPA, formerly employed by the IRS. After 10 years and three promotions, the most recent to Associate Director of Financial Planning and Analysis, she was terminated in February 2003.

Following what she describes as a period of daily abuse, she took medical leave in October 2002. Here's how she describes what happened next.

I was terminated on February 27, 2003. I am still on disability. I am afraid to go back to my field of work. I feel overwhelmed and frozen by the thought of re-entering this environment. Symptoms I suffer from include but are not limited to anxiety, depression, anger, shame, inability to concentrate, feelings of low self-esteem and low self-confidence, hyper-vigilance, and forgetfulness. I suffer from nightmares about my job, night sweats, irregular sleep patterns, isolation, and apprehension/fear of leaving the security of my home.

Due to my disability and inability to work, my husband and I are going to suffer the loss of our home. We are in the process of declaring bankruptcy and have no place to go.

I was terminated while on disability. I lost my health insurance for my family (three kids, myself, and my husband). I would have to pay $1,200 a month to continue our health insurance coverage under the Consolidated Omnibus Budget Reconciliation Act. My husband talked me into getting COBRA for myself so that I can access my therapist and my medication. I pay for this with my disability payments. We have stopped paying our mortgage and our credit cards.

If you do withdraw those funds, you'll be losing the opportunity to earn tax-deferred income on them. Plus, you'll be hit with income taxes on the withdrawal and, in all probability, a 10 percent penalty tax if you're younger than 59½. Note that if you've borrowed against your company-sponsored retirement plan, you will need to pay the loan back, usually within 45 to 90 days of your departure from the company, to avoid the loan being considered a withdrawal and thus subject to taxes and penalties.

Think of your retirement plan—whether IRA, Keogh, 401(k), or other pension plan—as truly your emergency stash. If you need funds, go to other places first. However, if you have a Roth IRA rather than a conventional one, you may have a bit more flexibility. You would incur a penalty if you withdrew funds from a conventional IRA, but a Roth IRA may allow you to withdraw your principal without any adverse tax consequences. Keep in mind that tax laws change frequently. Check with an expert before making any major moves.

Tapping into any personal savings or taxable investment accounts, even if you have to pay capital gains tax, is usually preferable to withdrawing money from your retirement plan. But what funds you access and how you access them depends upon a variety of factors including whether and how soon you plan to return to the job market.

DEFERRED COMPENSATION PLANS

If you participated in a plan that allowed you to defer compensation to a future date, typically until you retire, when you would presumably be in a lower marginal tax rate, your contributions to the plan are considered to be pretax income. Once you leave your job, and with it the deferred compensation plan, you generally will be required to take the entire value of your account as a lump-sum distribution. In some cases, however, participants may be eligible for monthly payouts or for some combination of a lump-sum distribution and regular payouts. Check with your plan administrator and your financial advisor to understand your options and take maximum advantage of them.

SEVERANCE PACKAGES

Unless you were very savvy or very senior, you may not have negotiated a severance package when you first accepted your position. If you have no severance package but are able to negotiate one prior to your departure, make sure the offer is in writing, review it carefully before signing, and make sure you get a copy properly signed by all parties. It is, after all, a legally binding contract. Consult with a qualified financial planner or attorney on any issues that are not clear or are not satisfactory.

Whatever the circumstances, if you are offered severance pay, you may need to choose whether to collect it over time or as a lump sum. Your decision will likely affect your tax bill. Spreading out the payments may prevent you from moving into a higher income-tax bracket for the year. On the other hand, if you accept another job while still receiving those periodic payments, they also could push you into a higher bracket. In all probability, though, the thought of making too much money is not on the top of your list of worries.

However, other factors may influence your decision. For example, you might want the lump sum if you plan to put the money into finding another job or starting your own business. Taking the payment in a lump sum also avoids the risk that the company might go bankrupt and not be able to make extended payments.

Alternatively, it may make more sense for you to take your severance pay over time if by doing so you can extend employee benefits such as healthcare coverage and retirement plan funding that might otherwise end immediately.

SOCIAL SECURITY

Your Social Security benefits, whether upon your retirement or through one of the two Social Security disability programs (See "Taking Action."), will provide you with only a portion of your previous income, very likely putting you in a lower tax bracket. As a consequence, you probably will hold on to a greater percentage of the income you receive when taxes come due.

However, although you may be paying less in taxes than you used to, you still will probably need more income than what you receive from Social Security. Thus, you'll want to first establish how much additional income you'll need and, second, find a way to make up the balance from your investments or other resources to maintain your standard of living.

If you're not eligible for one of the Social Security disability programs, consider taking early Social Security retirement benefits if you are 62 or older. However, first consult with your financial planner to determine if this is the best financial move, given your individual situation.

TAKING ACTION

Most of the discussion so far has been based on the assumption that you have not been living beyond your means, that your credit is not overextended, and that you do have some sort of financial base with which to work. If that's not the case, if you've been living in emotional turmoil and been hit with costly medical and/or legal fees, and/or if you don't have a partner or spouse who can help you through the tough times, you may have no choice but to take more dramatic action.

Even then, you can make a full recovery. First, step back and take a look at your situation as a whole. Make certain that you have indeed taken advantage of all of the employee benefits to which you are entitled, such as compensation for paid time off including accrued vacation and sick leave, any contributions you made to an employee pension plan, and the ability to extend your medical coverage through COBRA (See Chapter 12, "Protecting Your Health.") or a state or private equivalent.

Then, call in a professional. If you feel you can't afford the services of a qualified financial planner, call a reputable nonprofit organization such as the National Foundation for Credit Counseling, Consumer Counseling Centers of America, Myvcsta, or Alliance Credit Counseling. These organizations offer services ranging from consolidating debt and creating a budget to creditor mediation and bankruptcy avoidance. While many charge for some or all of their services, others do not. Before doing anything else, make sure the organization you choose is legitimate. Get a referral from someone you trust and/or check it out with the Better Business Bureau in your community or with your state's consumer fraud agency.

Although you may not yet be willing or able to face the job market yet, you may want to try some relatively low-stress alternatives. Check around for part-time and contract/freelance opportunities. The Internet is a tremendous resource for such positions (See the appendix for some useful links.). By taking on such work, which often can be done from home, you can begin rebuilding your self-confidence as well as your bank account.

EMERGENCY MEASURES

There's no denying that loss of income can be a devastating problem, and if you don't have resources to tap, you may have to take drastic measures and/or call on friends and family to help you through. But you can get through it. Some of the options you may want to consider include:

· Renting out a room in your home or taking in a roommate.

· Renting out your home or subletting your apartment, and renting a less-expensive residence. Perhaps you might also consider moving in with friends or relatives.

· Borrowing from a cash-value life insurance policy.

· Filing for bankruptcy.

· Withdrawing funds from a qualified retirement plan.

· Borrowing from family members or friends. If you go this route, it's usually a good idea to make the terms as formal and businesslike as possible in order to minimize the possibility of any confusion or disagreement down the road.

BORROWING FROM YOUR INSURANCE POLICY

If you own a cash-value (or permanent) life insurance policy, you probably bought it with the intention of securing long-term life insurance coverage. In addition to the coverage this life insurance provides, it has a cash value. This is because a portion of your premium goes into a savings account for your benefit. You can use this savings component, or "cash value," as a source of emergency income. Because the money you borrow is treated as debt rather than as a taxable distribution, you will owe no taxes on it. However, by tapping into it, you are reducing the funds that will be available to your beneficiaries.

DECLARING BANKRUPTCY

Declaring bankruptcy is not a step to take lightly. Fortunately, in

most cases, it's not a step you'll need to take at all. Before filing for
bankruptcy, make sure it's the appropriate choice. Learn all you
can about the process and the implications, and consult with family members, a bankruptcy attorney, and a qualified accountant.

Should you choose this route, you'll likely be selecting between
one of two options: Chapter 7 and Chapter 13 of the federal bankruptcy code. Chapter 7 bankruptcy, known as straight bankruptcy,
calls for the liquidation or sale of the debtor's nonexempt posses-
sions to repay creditors. Chapter 13 bankruptcy is sometimes called
wage-earner's bankruptcy because it calls for the debtor to repay the
debt in installments over time.

Under Chapter 7 bankruptcy, you would request a bankruptcy court to wipe out (or, more formally, to discharge) the bulk of
your debts, although not all of your debts can be discharged. In
turn, you will be required to sell some of your property, and the
sale proceeds will be used to pay off your creditors.

Some of the debts that cannot be discharged under either
Chapter 7 or a reorganization bankruptcy are secured debts such
as your mortgage or a car loan, child and spousal support payments, court fines and penalties, and certain student loans.

For more information about filing for personal bankruptcy,
check out Nolo Press for several helpful articles. Nolo also pub-
lishes several useful books on the topic, including *How to File for
Chapter 7 Bankruptcy* and *Bankruptcy: Is It the Right Solution to Your
Debt Problems?* Both are available through the Nolo Web site,
www.nolo.com, or from your bookstore.

ONCE YOU'VE FILED

Under Chapter 7—generally the option of choice for those who
decide to file for personal bankruptcy—you'll need to provide the
bankruptcy court with detailed financial information for the past
two years. At the time of filing, you'll be charged a fee, $200 at the
time of this writing, which may be waived if you are receiving public assistance or live below the legal poverty level. The court then
appoints a trustee to oversee your case.

Next, the trustee reviews your information and collects the
property that can be taken from you—called your nonexempt

property—to be sold to pay your creditors. Once you've done that you will, generally within six months, receive a court notice that all of your qualified debts have been discharged. That's it.

Reorganization under Chapter 13 of the bankruptcy code is more complicated. Basically, however, if your secured debt (debt that is guaranteed to be paid off with property) totals less than $871,550 and your other debts total less than $269,250, you can file for Chapter 13. In addition to providing your financial information, Chapter 13 requires you to file a proposal with the bankruptcy court explaining how you plan to repay your creditors over a given time period. The terms of payment will vary from creditor to creditor. You will not be required to repay all debts completely and some will not need to be repaid at all.

After meeting with the trustee and possibly some of your creditors as well to discuss your plan, your next step will be to attend a hearing before a bankruptcy judge who will decide whether to approve your plan. If it is approved and you make all the required payments, any balance owed at the end of your case may be discharged. In most states, you can protect at least 75 percent of wages you've earned but have not been paid.

Most people can keep their property when they file for bankruptcy, according to *Bankruptcy: Is It the Right Solution to Your Debt Problems?*[4] However, losing property in a bankruptcy filing is a possibility. For example, if you are behind in your mortgage payments and have filed a Chapter 7 bankruptcy, you could stand to lose your house or other property.

SO WHY NOT FILE?

Filing for bankruptcy may give you the time you need to get back on your feet financially. But while it may appear to be an easy way to get out of a financial bind, bankruptcy carries with it some significant consequences. If you declare bankruptcy, you will see that fact on your credit report for the next 10 years. That entry in your credit history can lead to other financial problems, such as the inability to get a loan for a car, a home mortgage, or even a credit card.

Moreover, while filing for bankruptcy may relieve you of some of your current financial burden, it will not help you to generate an income going forward. Instead, it can hinder you by show-ing up when a prospective employer chooses to check up on you (See Chapter 15, "The Second Time Around.").

GOVERNMENT ASSISTANCE

After reducing expenses, you may find that you still don't have the financial resources you need. If so, you may qualify for help from government or private agencies to tide you over until you're back on your feet. Depending on your circumstances, you may be eligi-ble for one or more state or federal benefit programs. Chances are the income you receive will be less than what you need to cover your expenses but enough to take the edge off of your situation.

A good place to start looking for the appropriate program for you is the Department of Health and Human Resources, which also provides a directory of state resources (See www.acf.hhs.gov/programs/ofa/hs_dir2.htm.). Eligibility for these programs may vary from state to state and from year to year, so to be sure to check with the relevant agency and/or a qualified professional for complete and up-to-date information.

ALTERNATIVES TO WORKERS' COMPENSATION

Even if your workers' compensation claim is successful, you may find yourself in a financial bind while waiting for your claim to kick in. If it isn't successful, that's all the more reason to check into your other options.

SOCIAL SECURITY DISABILITY

Contact your local Social Security office to find out if you are eli-gible to collect disability (See Chapter 10, "Getting Fired and Other Exits."). For you to be eligible, your condition must be severe enough that it interferes with the basic work-related activi-ties of your prior employment. Further you must be unable to do any other work. Factors that will come into play include your med-ical condition, age, education, past work experience, and transfer-able skills.

Collecting Social Security benefits may affect your ability to collect workers' compensation. A general rule of thumb is that your Social Security and workers' compensation benefits combined can't exceed 80 percent of your average earnings just prior to the onset of your disability. Your ability to collect Social Security disability benefits may also be affected by civil service disability benefits, state temporary disability benefits, and state or local government retirement benefits based on disability.

UNEMPLOYMENT COMPENSATION

Check with your local unemployment office to find out if you can collect unemployment benefits while you're waiting for your workers' compensation claim to start paying. Eligibility varies on a state-by-state basis, and a combination of state and federal laws determines who is eligible, how much you receive, and how long benefits last. Generally, you must be able and willing to do a specific type of work and be able to demonstrate that you are actively seeking employment (See Chapter 10, "Getting Fired and Other Exits.").

HEALTH INSURANCE

One of the things you can't afford to do during this period is to put your health—either physical or mental—at risk. As a consequence, making certain that you have appropriate health insurance coverage should be a high priority (See Chapter 12, "Protecting Your Health.").

SHORT-TERM DISABILITY INSURANCE

Only a few states, including California, Hawaii, New Jersey, New York, and Rhode Island, have state-sponsored disability programs. These programs are typically short term and the benefit amounts are usually low (See Chapter 12, "Protecting Your Health.").

CREDIT OR MORTGAGE INSURANCE

If you've ever signed up for supplemental insurance through a credit card or mortgage company, now is the time to dig up the paperwork and read the fine print—it just might cover a disability, temporary or otherwise. Having your credit card or mortgage payments covered, even for a short period of time, could make your financial situation a lot more manageable.

ADA ACCOMMODATIONS

Your employer may be obligated to bring you back to do work you can currently handle. Check out the Americans with Disabilities Act accommodation requirements.

WORKERS' COMPENSATION AND SOCIAL SECURITY

As noted earlier, if you receive disability payments from a workers' compensation (See Chapter 11, "Workers' Compensation.") or other public disability payment, your Social Security benefits probably will be reduced to reflect those payments. In other words, your Social Security benefit together with your workers' compensation payment and/or public disability payment cannot exceed 80 percent of your average earnings prior to your disability. However, although you may receive less than the full benefit in order to stay under that 80 percent maximum, you will nevertheless need to report the unreduced benefit on your income taxes.

Depending on your situation, if your workers' compensation claim succeeds, one of a variety of entities may be responsible for paying it, including federal or state workers' compensation agencies, employers, or insurance companies on behalf of employers.

Unlike workers' compensation, public disability payments, which may be paid under a federal, state, or local government law or plan, do not require that your disability be job-related. Examples of such payments include civil service disability benefits, military disability benefits, state temporary disability benefits, and state or local government retirement benefits based on disability.

If you think you may qualify for such payments, call or email the relevant agency and discuss your situation with your doctor as well as your accountant to ensure that you are receiving all that you are entitled to, and are not setting yourself up for any unwelcome surprises from the IRS.

If the work you did to earn federal, state, or local government benefits was covered by Social Security, those benefits will not reduce your Social Security benefit. In addition, Veterans Administration benefits, private pension payments, private insurance payments, and Supplemental Security Income (SSI) payments will not affect your Social Security benefit. As always, however, these regulations change. Check with the relevant government agency to make sure you have the most up-to-date information before taking any action.

Social Security pays disability benefits under two programs. The first is the Social Security Disability Insurance Program, which pays benefits to you and certain members of your family if you have worked long enough and have paid Social Security taxes. The second program is the SSI program, which is based on financial need. But for your claim to be considered under either program, your condition must interfere with basic work-related activities. In addition, to qualify for benefits, your previous employment must include jobs covered by Social Security. And, hardly surprisingly, you must have a medical condition that meets Social Security's definition of disability, which, in general, encompasses people who are unable to work for a year or more because of a disability.

The monthly cash benefits usually continue until you are able to work again on a regular basis. If you return to work, you may be entitled to "reasonable accommodations" by your employer if they are necessary to enable you to do your job effectively. However, your employer may not need to make those accommodations if it can establish that doing so would constitute a hardship.

If you are receiving Social Security disability benefits when you reach age 65, your disability benefits automatically convert to retirement benefits. The benefit amount remains the same. More information is available at www.ssa.gov.

8.

BULLYING AND THE LAW

The material presented in this chapter and elsewhere in the book is
intended to offer a general overview of bullying and the law. It is in
no way intended to substitute for professional legal advice, and
should in no way be regarded as legal advice. Please note, too, that
the law in your state and/or local jurisdiction may differ from the
laws described herein. Consult a qualified attorney before taking
legal action.

Your employer can shower you with sarcasm and contempt,
deriding your every move, questioning your competence, doubting
your intelligence, sneering at you in public, yelling at you in private. He may in fact, be the most irritating individual ever to walk
the earth. But being obnoxious, boorish, rude, and even sadistic, is
not against the law, unless some very carefully drawn lines are
crossed in the process.

LEGAL ACTION: AN OVERVIEW

Many people who have experienced bullying or other abusive
behavior in the workplace assume that, if they have been treated
badly, they have the basis for a successful lawsuit. As reasonable as
that assumption may seem, however, that is not necessarily the
case. As an employee who has left or is prepared to leave an abusive workplace, you have a number of legal remedies to consider.
However, none of them may prove to be applicable to your situation, especially if the abuse you faced did not stem from discrimination on the basis of your gender, nationality, race, religion, age
group, or disability as defined by law.

At present, there is no law on the books that specifically

deals with "equal opportunity" bullying—behavior that, while not technically violating anti-discrimination laws, is nevertheless abusive. Although there are some instances in which a link to a so-called protected class does not need to be established, any time you and your attorney can create such a tie, your position is likely to strengthen.

Should you decide to move forward with a lawsuit, you need to keep in mind that none of your legal options is likely to be either simple, swift, or cheap, either monetarily or emotionally.

Unfortunately, if you're dealing with an "equal opportunity" bully, although your manager's behavior may be obnoxious and, in many cases, damaging, it most likely is not unlawful. And if it is unlawful, it may be difficult to prove. In the western US, however, some lawmakers are working to extend the protections offered by legislation such as Title VII of the Civil Rights Act of 1964, which outlaws discriminations based on race, color, religion, sex, or national origin. The Americans with Disabilities Act and the Age Discrimination in Employment Act may also apply to targets of bullying (See Chapter 17, "Legal Directions.").

In the meantime, unless you are able to establish a connection between your case and one of the specific classes recognized by current federal law, you may be better off forgetting the lawsuit, and working on getting on with your life.

If, on the other hand, you can make even a tenuous connection, you and your attorney may decide to go forward in the hope of finding a sympathetic jury or reaching an out-of-court settlement.

CAUSES FOR ACTION

Broadly speaking, most lawsuits alleging emotional or psychological harm as a result of abusive workplace behavior require a connection to federal discrimination laws, discussed below. More specifically, employees seeking legal redress for such abuse generally seek to establish either intentional infliction of emotional distress or wrongful termination, encompassing constructive discharge, retaliation and discrimination, as well as breach of contract—a cause of action typically not available to at-will employees. The bulk of the US working population is employed "at-will."

At-will employment refers to an employment relationship wherein the employer has the right to terminate an individual's employment for any cause at any time, with or without notice. That is, unless you are a union member covered by a labor agreement or a member of senior management employed under a formal contract, you are probably an "at-will" employee.

DISCRIMINATION

To succeed with a claim of discrimination, you'll need to have a legally recognized claim based on a protected category as defined under federal legislation such as Title VII of the Civil Rights Act of 1964, the Americans with Disabilities Act and the Age Discrimination in Employment Act.

However, even though "non-protected" abuse is not addressed by any statute, if you can establish a link between the abuse and one of the protected characteristics, you may have a case, suggests attorney James Stoneman. For instance, if your manager uses profanity that you find offensive and which can be tied to gender, racial, or age discrimination, even if you're not a member of the protected class, you may have a case, Stoneman says. If you can't make that link, you will not be able to succeed with a discrimination suit. [1]

INTENTIONAL INFLICTION OF

EMOTIONAL DISTRESS (IIED)

Intentional infliction of emotional distress has been defined by the courts as extreme and outrageous conduct that not only is intended to cause but does cause severe emotional distress to another.

In order to win a suit based on a claim of IIED, you'll need to establish that not only was your bully's conduct intentional or reckless, but that his behavior was so extravagant and unacceptable that it contravened generally accepted standards of decency and morality. Unfortunately, there's no clear definition of just what those "generally accepted" standards might be. Additionally, you must establish that your bully is, in fact, the cause of your emotional distress. Emotional distress in this context means severe emotional distress. Of course, the word "severe" is also open to differing interpretations.

If you claim intentional infliction of emotional distress, your claim does not need to be linked to a protected class. A lawsuit based on IIED enables you, as the plaintiff, to sue for emotional distress and punitive damages. However, IIED is very difficult to prove. "The intentional infliction of emotional distress must be truly extreme," notes Florida attorney and arbitration specialist Don Spero. "Moreover, you must be able to support your case with extremely compelling and well-documented evidence, if the allegation is to be found valid by a court."[2]

If your manager's bullying behavior causes you to fear violence from him, you may have grounds for a related claim of assault or attempted assault. Similarly, unwanted physical contact may lay the basis for a claim of battery. If your manager has threatened you in any way, talk to your attorney about your legal options and, if you have one, your union rep, about your out-of-court choices.

While allegations of intentional infliction of emotional distress don't need to be tied to a protected class recognized under federal law, they are very difficult to establish without that link. Oregon attorney Paul Buchanan estimates that 90 percent of all IIED claims made are dismissed.[3]

To win a suit for negligent infliction of emotional distress, you will need to prove not only that your manager engaged in such conduct, but that your employer could reasonably foresee that such conduct would cause you severe emotional distress or mental anguish. Finally, you then must prove that the conduct did indeed cause severe emotional distress.

If you succeeded in proving intentional infliction of emotional distress, you could receive punitive damages for your bully's actions. Unlike compensatory damages, which are intended to compensate the actual loss that you, as the plaintiff, have suffered as a consequence of your bully's conduct, punitive damages are intended to punish the defendant and to deter repetition of the wrongful conduct. However, even if you can help your case along by establishing your "protected status" under the law, you may discover that you lack sufficient grounds for a decision in your favor.

According to attorney Michael Sorgen, employers recently gained an additional defense against IIED claims. Known as a "good-faith personnel action," this defense basically holds that no grounds for litigation exist if an employer has criticized an employee for not performing if the criticism is deemed to have been made in good faith—that is, if the employer can demonstrate that he believed his comments to be valid and that they were made without any attempt to deceive.

WRONGFUL TERMINATION

In *Dillard Department Stores, Inc., v. Gonzales*, the Eighth Court of Appeals in El Paso County, Texas, ruled on March 7, 2002, that "to recover damages for intentional infliction of emotional distress, a plaintiff must prove: (1) the defendant acted intentionally or recklessly, (2) the defendant's conduct was extreme and outrageous, (3) the defendant's actions caused the plaintiff emotional distress, and (4) the resulting emotional distress suffered by the plaintiff was severe."

Wrongful termination comes in several different flavors, none of them particularly appetizing. Under certain circumstances, a claim of wrongful termination may apply if your employer fired or laid you off, or forced you to quit or retire. If you are pressing a claim of wrongful termination on the basis of discrimination, harassment, or retaliation, it must be successfully linked to your standing as a member of a "protected class." That would be discrimination, and discrimination is illegal.

In other words, if you are an at-will employee, your employer can fire you because he doesn't like you, but he cannot fire you if he doesn't like you because you are a member of one of the classes protected by law. However, if you are employed under the terms of a contract, a breach of that contract doesn't necessarily have to be linked to federal discrimination law. Thus, even if you don't have a contract, your employer can't legally terminate your employment solely on the basis of your gender, race, age, disability, or other reasons set forth in federal law.

Similarly, a lawsuit based on allegations of harassment or a hostile work environment typically must be tied to federally protected categories such as race, sex, physical disability, or religion protected under Title VII of the Civil Rights Act of 1964, or a related act.

However, Paul Buchanan notes that the courts are increasingly finding that discriminatory harassment does not need to be explicitly linked to sex, gender, race, or other protected characteristics. Instead, discriminatory harassment can consist simply of bad conduct that has been prompted by the presence of a protected characteristic.[4]

In 1999 in the case *Meritor Savings Bank v. Vinson*, the Sixth Circuit Court found that unequal treatment of an employee that occurred only because of the employee's gender or other protected characteristic could "if sufficiently severe or pervasive" constitute a hostile environment in violation of federal law. Under this interpretation, then, even if your boss's bullying is not explicitly sexist in nature, you still may be able to make your case by arguing that had you been male (or female, as the case may be), you would not have been subject to harassment by your manager.

Buchanan uses an example of an employer's policy of not hiring individuals who have custody of pre-school age children. That policy in itself may or may not be deemed discriminatory. However, if the effect of the policy is to screen out a disproportionate number of women from possible employment, it would be considered to have an "adverse impact"[5] on those women, and so could be considered to be discriminatory under Title VII.

If you try that test at your workplace and discover that virtually all of the bully's targets were of one gender, you may be able to make the argument that gender harassment was at work. However, if, for example, you are the only individual that your bully currently has in his sights, but that he has in the past bullied each of your predecessors regardless of gender, your "protected claim" probably wouldn't work.

CAN YOU SUE FOR WRONGFUL TERMINATION?

The following are some examples of several major areas in which the courts have held that employees can successfully sue for wrongful termination, despite an explicit or implicit "at-will" clause:

·   Violation of the law or public policy. If you are fired for refusing to carry out an order (insubordination) that you can demonstrate violates state or federal law, or commonly accepted standards of morality and ethics.

·   Violation of promise of fair dealing. A violation of a

promise of "fair dealing" is another instance in which the at-will employment rule does not apply. In other words, if you can prove that your employer made you a promise, either explicit or implied, and later revoked it unilaterally and without consideration to you, you may be able to prove a claim of wrongful termination.

· Constructive discharge. Despite your at-will employment status, if you can show that you resigned effectively because your employer rendered working conditions so intolerable that no reasonable person would continue to work in the environment, then you essentially are deemed to have been fired.

Because of its somewhat amorphous nature, constructive discharge, particularly when not related to a protected class, is extremely difficult to prove. However, it can be done. Arguing that she had been constructively discharged, a human resources manager successfully sued a California employer for "yelling and screaming" in the workplace. In *Thompson v. Tracor Flight Systems*, the HR manager challenged her supervisor's work orders because implementing those orders would have violated California employment law. She complained to both the supervisor and senior management that her supervisor—who had given the order—repeatedly yelled at her over the course of several months, often in front of the entire office. These outbursts eventually became so violent that the HR manager "feared for her safety,"[6] and later resigned, claiming constructive discharge.

After hearing the case, the court ruled that these working conditions were "unusually aggravated"[7] and amounted to a continuous pattern deemed to be intolerable for the employee and which the employer refused to correct or mitigate. The court awarded the HR manager $600,000 based on the wrongful termination.

This case highlights the view of an increasing number of courts that all employees are entitled to a reasonable workplace, free of harassment and negative treatment.

RETALIATION

Retaliation refers to any adverse action that your employer takes against you because you complained about harassment, discrimination, or some other violation of a work-related law, or if you are fired because you blew the whistle on an illegal activity or participated in an investigation of such an activity.

That means that if you lose your original suit against your employer for another claim and are subsequently fired as a result of that claim, you now may have new grounds for a lawsuit. Thus, while often tied to a protected class, that protected class status is not necessary to a claim of retaliation.

Moreover, you can make a claim of retaliation even if you are not fired, but are subjected to hostile behavior, demotion, discipline, salary reduction, a negative evaluation, a change in job assignment, or change in shift assignment for these activities.

A recent example of unlawful termination due to retaliation is *Shellenberger v. Summit Bancorp. Inc.*, in which the plaintiff had asked for a series of accommodations related to her "perfume sensitivity." The defendant had concluded that the employee did not have a disability as defined by the ADA but had nevertheless attempted to satisfy her concerns by taking several measures, none of which resolved the problem. In an effort at accommodation, the employer moved her desk several times, allowed her to keep a fan on her desk, and arranged to have a supervisor whose perfume bothered the employee discuss business matters over the telephone, rather than in person.

Ultimately, however, none of that worked. The defendant decided that it could not satisfy the employee's demands and, based on the premise that the employee was not protected under the ADA, the employer terminated the plaintiff's employment for insubordination, claiming that she had accused her employer of poisoning her and that her requests were framed as ultimatums.

Although lower courts found no fault with the employer's decision, the Third Circuit Court ultimately ruled that there was sufficient evidence to conclude that the employer had in fact fired the plaintiff in retaliation for actions protected by the ADA. According to the court, regardless of whether an individual establishes that a covered disability exists, the ADA protects any employee who files a good faith claim. Therefore, the Third Circuit Court concluded, to proceed on a retaliation claim, a plaintiff does not need to be a "qualified individual with a disability"[8] under the ADA. Instead, it found that status under the ADA is not relevant in assessing the person's claim for retaliation under the ADA.

In other words, under this decision, if you make a "good faith" request for accommodation under federal legislation, no retaliatory action can be taken against you for making that request, even if a court ultimately finds that you are not eligible for the requested accommodation.

WHISTLE A HAPPY TUNE

In general terms, a whistleblower is an employee who challenges corporate and government abuses of power that betray the public trust. Whistleblowing may include reporting wrongdoing or a violation of the law to the proper authorities, refusing to participate in workplace wrongdoing, testifying in a legal proceeding, or leaking evidence of wrongdoing to the media.

Whistleblower claims have specific protections under federal and, in many instances, state law. For example, if you report your employer to the police or a state or federal agency for some violation (even if the allegation is subsequently not proved), your company may not be able to fire you because of the report, even if you are an at-will employee, which you very likely may be.

A CLOSER LOOK AT AT-WILL EMPLOYMENT

As mentioned before, most employment in the US is categorized as "at-will." The caveat to this is that while the "cause" for firing may be trivial or even silly, it cannot be unlawful. Even more broadly, according to Cameron and Morgan Reynolds, writing in the July 2003 issue of *The Cato Review of Business & Government*, a handful of states are requiring employers to demonstrate that a firing was not a violation of public policy, a breach of implied contract, or a private tort. (A tort can be defined as an injury to an individual for which another individual is legally responsible.)[9] Thus in California, for example, courts have held that an employee may not be terminated if the employee's dismissal contradicts "fundamental" and "established" public policy.[10]

In a suit for wrongful termination, you may sue your former employer for damages, typically representing your total compensation package. In addition, you may also sue for attorneys' fees, back pay, reinstatement, and emotional distress. If your termination is also established to be not only "wrongful," but illegal or contrary to public policy, your former employer may also be liable for punitive damages. That means that you may be able to successfully sue for wrongful termination even if you earlier had agreed to and signed an "at-will" provision, provided that you can show that your employer's action violated state or federal law, or violated public policy.

If you are an at-will employee who has been terminated, it may be worth your while to check for company policies or documentation that may modify that relationship. For example, your company's employee handbook could prove to be an unexpected ally if you're contemplating legal action. In committing to, for example, a professional, positive work environment, the handbook may well prohibit the very type of behavior that your bully displays. You then may have a legal claim for breach of contract, even though it's not discrimination under federal law.

In addition, memos or performance reviews implying that you're being considered for a promotion or a raise could be construed as an implicit contract. If you suspect this may be your situation, check with your attorney. However, while this approach is worth investigating with your attorney, don't be surprised if your employee handbook and other employee materials are so vague and so laden with disclaimers as to be useless to you. You may even discover that, when you first began the job, you signed a waiver of some of your rights without realizing it.

HOSTILE WORK ENVIRONMENT CLAIM

To establish a hostile work environment claim, you may have to establish that the conduct to which you have been subjected has unreasonably interfered with your work performance or created an intimidating, hostile, or offensive work environment. However, once again, the harassment to which you've been subjected may need to be based on race, gender, or other protected characteristics and be so severe and pervasive that it has unreasonably interfered with your work performance and created an abusive atmosphere.

Although the conduct at issue can be that of anyone employed by the company, whether a supervisor, coworker, or contractor, you must be able to demonstrate that your employer has some responsibility for the abusive workplace environment. That is, in most cases, your employer would be liable for hostile work environment harassment by those in its employ only if it actually knew of the harassment or if it could have learned of the harassment and failed to take immediate and appropriate action to correct it.

The hostile work environment claim was originally intended to address harassment that was sexual in nature. More recently, some courts have broadened the definition to include other protected categories. In 2001, for example, in *Fox v. General Motors Corp.*, a federal appeals court ruled that a plaintiff can claim a hostile work environment under the Americans with Disabilities Act, while in other instances, the Fourth and Fifth Circuit Courts of Appeals, relying on case law interpreting Title VII, also held that hostile work environment claims are available under the ADA.[11]

But, although your workplace may be an extraordinarily unfriendly one, the courts have so far confined the hostile workplace doctrine to characteristics defined under Title VII, the ADA, and the Age Discrimination in Employment Act (ADEA) of 1967. Thus, once again, unless your argument is in some way tied to one of the protected classes, a hostile workplace claim is virtually impossible to establish under current law.

As with all such litigation, though, if your attorney explores beneath the surface, she may find the necessary link. For instance, if the hostility is directed primarily or solely toward men while women are treated relatively cordially, you may have—perhaps not enough to win a case—but enough to reach an out-of-court settlement.

Even if the claim is tied to a protected characteristic, to rise to the level of a hostile work environment, the harassment typically cannot consist of isolated incidents, but must recur over an extended period. As a consequence, sporadic incidents of flirting or telling off-color jokes may not constitute sexual harassment.

To establish a hostile work environment claim, you don't need to prove that you have incurred direct economic harm, but you must provide persuasive evidence that the conduct at issue was not only malicious and recurring, but also severe and/or pervasive.

CONSTRUCTIVE DISCHARGE

Generally, a court will find that a constructive discharge has occurred when working conditions are so intolerable that a reasonable person would feel compelled to resign. The paper trail you've created documenting run-ins with your bully can go a long way in helping to establish your case. Establishing the existence of such conditions is akin to proving a hostile workplace claim except, in this instance, you do not necessarily have to link the harassment to a protected class. However, your case would doubtless be easier to make if such a connection could be established.

Like intentional infliction of emotional distress, the circumstances surrounding "constructive discharge" must truly be extreme and documented by significant, legally acceptable evidence.

Determining whether a "reasonable" employee would feel forced to resign is a subjective decision, and must be decided anew in accordance with the unique facts of each case. However, when determining whether constructive discharge has occurred, courts typically consider events such as demotion; salary cuts; reduced job responsibilities; reassignment to menial or degrading work; and badgering, harassment, or humiliation. Other factors may include offers of early retirement or of continued employment on terms less favorable than the employee's former status. But while any or all of these factors may be considered, none guarantees that the court will conclude that a constructive discharge has taken place.

According to Florida attorney and mediator Donald J. Spero, an employee's resignation also may be deemed to be a constructive discharge if the employer obtains the resignation by coercion or deception.[1][2] The court's determination of whether you were constructively discharged is likely to depend on factors such as whether your employer's conduct in obtaining your resignation deprived you of choice. In other words, your only option was to resign. The court will also look to see whether you had a reasonable period in which you could make your decision as well as a voice in choosing the effective date of your resignation. Under some circumstances, if you did not have the advice of counsel at the time of your resignation, your constructive discharge argument may stand a better chance.

In the 1996 decision *Bristow v. Daily Press, Inc.*, a circuit court found that an employee is "protected from a calculated effort to pressure him into resignation through the imposition of unreasonably harsh conditions, in excess of those faced by his coworkers. He is not, however, guaranteed a working environment free of stress."[13]

DO YOU HAVE A CLAIM UNDER ADEA?

The Age Discrimination in Employment Act of 1967 protects individuals who are 40 years of age or older from employment discrimination based on age. The ADEA's protections apply to both employees and job applicants. Under the ADEA, it is unlawful to discriminate against a person because of his/her age with respect to any term, condition, or privilege of employment including but not limited to hiring, firing, promotion, layoffs, compensation benefits, job assignments, and training.

The ADEA applies to employers, including state and local governments, with 20 or more employees. It also applies to employment agencies and to labor organizations as well as to the federal government.

Once you understand the various legal options open to you, and have discussed them with your attorney, the next step is to determine whether you want to embark on the long and often arduous task of pressing a legal claim against your bully.

Again, the material provided here is intended for general informational purposes only. Before taking any legal action, make sure to consult a qualified attorney and consider all of the pertinent factors involved.

9.

YOUR DAY IN COURT?

Because non-generic abusive management is not addressed by any statute, you need to determine whether the conduct is some form of discriminatory harassment under one of the protected categories. Frequently we find that it is. If you look a little further, you will find that the abuse is somehow tied to one of the protected characteristics. You need to find out what's really happening in the workplace.
—*James Stoneman, Esq.*

Unless you can establish that your manager's action was illegal under legislation such as Title VII of the Civil Rights Act of 1964, the Americans with Disabilities Act, or the Age Discrimination in Employment Act solidly enough to win an out-of-court settlement, if not a lawsuit, you may be better off hanging on to your money and focusing your energies outside of the courtroom.

Unfortunately, being right is not always enough. Even if you belong to one of the so-called protected classes enumerated in federal law, winning your case is not going to be easy. If you signed an employment agreement, you may be bound to turn to arbitration rather than to the court system. Or, if you choose not to go to court, you may instead want to consider the possibility of mediation (See Chapter 10, "Getting Fired and Other Exits," for more on both these options.).

Nevertheless, once you start down the path toward a lawsuit, your former employer may offer an out-of-court settlement. Indeed, by pressing ahead with a lawsuit, you may prompt your employer to at least attempt to negotiate a settlement. Many times, even if the plaintiff's evidence is not overwhelming, a defendant may choose to settle rather than to confront the expense, bother, and possible adverse publicity that could result from a trial.

Again, you'll need to carefully weigh the benefits and disadvantages of a settlement versus continuing with your case, and consult an attorney for advice. In any event, you should know what you will and will not accept well before you start the legal wheels in motion.

If you have sustained a significant disability from your experience, another option is to file a stress-related workers' compensation claim (See Chapter 11, "Workers' Compensation."). Should you decide to go this route, your attorney will probably agree to work with you on a contingency basis. If your attorney takes your case on contingency, he'll get a percentage of any monetary award you win. If you lose, you will still need to pay court costs as well as reimburse your lawyer for costs incurred on your behalf, including postage, photocopies, long-distance phone calls, witness fees, etc.

BEFORE YOU START

If you are contemplating litigation, getting everything in writing and/or verified by a witness can mean the difference between winning and losing your case. If you're still on the job and considering litigation, avoid speaking to your boss without a witness. If you are in a public place where no "expectation of privacy" exists, attorney Don Sessions suggests that taping the exchange could mean the difference between a clear-cut victory and a case in which it's your word against his. However, be certain to check with your attorney before you tape a conversation without the other party's knowledge, as this may be illegal in your state.

While you may be eager to walk off of your job, you may have reason to wait if you're planning to sue. Discuss your options with an attorney before you act. You may choose to stick around for the chance to see what your boss does next—his further inappropriate action may provide an opportunity to submit an additional claim and request that your boss resolve it within a stated time period. If this happens and he doesn't respond, you then may have the basis for a claim of wrongful termination through constructive discharge. And that may be the time to walk off the job.

As you start to pull together arguments and evidence for your case, keep in mind that there are occasions in which the fight is just not worth the effort, and where the best course of action may be simply to move on with your life.

LEGAL (AND OTHER) COSTS

Before you take any definitive steps toward a lawsuit, make sure that you not only have the appropriate professionals firmly in your corner, but that you are aware of and willing to deal with the emotional and financial costs of pursuing litigation. If you don't have a lawyer who specializes in employment issues, start screening candidates right away. Make sure you find someone who makes you feel comfortable and who is sympathetic to and knowledgeable about your situation. If you don't have someone in mind, the National Employment Lawyers Association (www.nela.org) can refer you to an employment attorney in your state. The American Bar Association also can refer you to a qualified attorney (www.abanet.org).

In addition, you may want to contact your state bar association or check one of the legal directories available online. Lawyers are licensed to practice on a state-by-state basis, so the individual you choose must be licensed in the state where the case will be filed. The following are a few of the directories available online:

· AllLaw.com (www.alllaw.com) provides links to law firm Web sites that have chosen to be listed.

· The Employment Lawyer Directory (www.the-eld.com) offers an online "lawyer locater," and will also take information you provide, and cross reference it against its database to see if it can find a "match."

· FindLaw (www.findlaw.com) provides search tools to help you locate legal professionals in your location, or by specific practice area.

· Lawyers.com (www.lawyers.com), a service from Martindale-Hubbell, offers a free database of attorneys nationwide searchable by area of practice, geographical location, and other characteristics, and "Ask a Lawyer," an interactive forum for submitting legal questions to an attorney.

·   MyEmploymentLawyer.com (www.myemployment-lawyer.com) is a network of employment lawyers across the United States who represent individual employees. This site provides access to employment law attorneys online, as well as employment-law-related FAQs, forums, and answers to specific legal questions.

·   WorkplaceLawyer.com (www.workplacelawyer.com) offers a nationwide listing of employment lawyers who have public Web sites featuring their law practices. Most attorneys listed are members of NELA and primarily represent employees.

With the exception of workers' compensation claims, which attorneys typically take on a contingency basis, for most work-related litigation, the attorney you choose will probably charge an hourly fee in addition to reimbursable expenses. The fee charged will depend on a variety of factors, including the lawyer's experience, the prestige of the firm, and any support staff he brings in to assist.

Before you commit to legal action, take a hard look at the emotional and financial price you're likely to incur. In addition to assessing the facts of your case, you should also consider a number of additional factors, including:

·   Attorneys' fees.

·   Doctors' fees, e.g., therapists who will be testifying on your behalf, not to mention the extra hours of therapy you may need to help you deal with the stress attached to a lawsuit.

·   Downtime. The value of your time devoted to the conflict, that is, how much revenue could you have earned had your time and energy not been taken up by litigation.

·   Health costs. In addition to the medical bills you incur, factor in the stress you'll experience.

Don't be surprised if your attorney tells you that you don't have sufficient grounds to pursue your claim. Keep in mind that despite whatever injustices you suffered, you very likely may not have a persuasive case under current law. Don't get discouraged. He's doing you a favor by telling it to you straight if you do not have compelling legal evidence. Similarly, your attorney may decline to represent you in your workers' compensation claim if he feels your evidence is not overwhelming.

You, of course, have the option of obtaining a second, third, or even fourth opinion. You may need to find someone out of the ordinary who has the creativity to forge the link between your dilemma and a strong claim. Then again, your case may simply not be strong enough in today's legal environment.

If you're persuaded that your case is sufficiently solid, and you have found an attorney you want to represent you, you still must determine that you're financially able to have your day in court.

Although your first visit to an attorney is often, but not always, free, the ones that follow assuredly are not. Before you make that first appointment, get as much information about the attorney's fees and policies as you can. Make a list of all of your questions. If you haven't talked much about your experience, be prepared for your interview to be upsetting as you review all of the details. If you don't feel comfortable with the attorney after your first experience, don't hesitate to begin talking to other lawyers. Make sure you find the right one. Ideally, you'll find an attorney who has experience with and sympathy for victims of "equal opportunity abusers."

If you feel that the attorney's fees and related expenses are more than you can handle, check with your local legal aid society to see if it is able to represent you or help you find an affordable attorney. Again, you'll want to find out what other charges you are likely to incur. You'll also want to find out as much as you can with regard to the effort that the attorney anticipates the case will involve and what he expects from you. Talk to him about doing some of the legwork yourself as part of your effort to keep your legal expenses under control.

Also ask the attorney if he will require a retainer and, if so, how much. Get as much detail as you can, including the purposes for which the retainer will be used, whether the money will be returned to you if there's a balance, how the balance will be used, and whether you will owe money if the retainer is exhausted.

Request an estimate of the total cost, but recognize that it will be only an estimate. You'll also want to get a signed fee agreement that details how you will be charged. A fee agreement normally includes the hourly rates billed and the billing frequency.

In addition, you'll want to find out how frequently you should expect status letters and other communications, including billing statements, from the attorney. To keep costs down, request that copies of all correspondence and court documents routinely be sent to you without a cover letter. Paying copying and postage will be far less expensive than frequent updates from the attorney by letter or phone.

ARE YOU PROTECTED BY THE ADA?

To be eligible for protection under the Americans with Disabilities Act, you must have a disability as defined by the ADA. Under the act, you have a disability if you have a physical or mental impairment that substantially limits a major life activity such as hearing, seeing, speaking, thinking, walking, breathing, or performing manual tasks. You also must be able to do the job you want or were hired to do, with or without "reasonable accommodation."

Reasonable accommodation, as defined by the US Department of Labor, refers to any modification or adjustment to a job or work environment that will enable a qualified applicant or employee with a disability to participate in the application process or to perform essential job functions. Reasonable accommodation also includes adjustments to ensure that a qualified individual with a disability has rights and privileges in employment equal to those of employees without disabilities. For more information, visit www.usdoj.gov/crt/ada/workta.htm.

If you call a lawyer with questions, remember that your call is on the clock. To control this time, make a list of your questions so you don't forget anything and stick to the subject while you're talking to him. In fact, you may want to write him a letter or send him an email instead. It's liable to prove less time-consuming and, thus, less expensive. Plus it will give your attorney an instant record of your thoughts and comments for future reference. And ask about other expenses your attorney anticipates. For example, your attorney may need to hire a court reporter to take a deposition, a sworn statement of a witness in your case.

If you don't need the attorney's advice or opinion, speak to his paralegal or secretary instead. They cannot provide legal advice, but they can advise you of the status of your case, help you with scheduling, confirm that a letter has been received or written, and provide other information that does not involve a legal opinion.

10.

GETTING FIRED AND OTHER EXITS

"'You're fired!' No other words can so easily and succinctly reduce a confident, self-assured executive to an insecure, groveling shred of his former self. Or, handled creatively, getting fired allows an executive ... to actually experience a sense of relief that he never wanted the job he has lost."
—*Frank P. Louchheim, Chairman, Right Associates, from* Simpson's Contemporary Quotations

Getting fired is almost always traumatic, a direct blow to your self esteem. But it's by no means a fatal blow, and may just prove to be the best thing that happened to you.

Okay, so that last sounds like it's straight from the Pollyanna school of philosophy. But it may nonetheless be true. Consider the toll that your bullying manager and toxic workplace have taken on you, undermining your health and your self-esteem. You no longer have to go to work each morning dreading a conversation with your manager or constantly wondering where the bully's next strike will come from.

Still, depending on the specific circumstances of your departure, you may feel depressed or embarrassed about being fired. You may feel as if you have failed at a task at which you should have succeeded. You may be angry or frustrated with your former employer. Or you may just feel poor.

All of these are natural responses to the situation. And you should allow yourself to feel them, and deal with them, so that you can move on.

TURNING THE TABLES

If you have been let go or suspect that you're about to be, you may still have some leverage over your former employer. If you're a federal employee, you can file a complaint if you feel your firing reflects discrimination based on any of the traditional protected categories such as gender, race, age, disability, national origin, etc. Your complaint should be filed with your agency's internal Equal Employment Opportunity Commission (EEOC). For more information, visit the EEOC on the Web at www.eeoc.gov/facts/fs-fed.html.

If your complaint deals with mistreatment or unfairness unrelated to one of the protected categories, you may want to investigate sending a complaint to the Merit System Protection Board (MSPB). You can find more information about the MSPB's appeals process at www.mspb.gov/foia/forms-pubs/qaappeal.html.

If you are employed in the private sector, you may want to review any sources of information you have with regard to employment law, wrongful termination, retaliation, and discrimination, including the resources listed in the appendix.

Before you decide to go to court, consider all of your options. If your employer has an internal grievance process, you might want to start there. But be aware that your state may have a statute of limitations restricting your ability to file a wrongful termination lawsuit or take other avenues that may be open to you.

Also, be aware that, just as they say on TV, anything you say—a remark made while you're upset, a statement taken out of context—may be used against you in court if you do file a lawsuit.

If you believe you were fired under circumstances that were discriminatory, you may want to file a complaint with the Equal Employment Opportunity Commission, which will review your case without charge. You can contact the EEOC by telephone at 800-669-4000 or 800-669-6820 (TDD). For additional information, see www.eeoc.gov.

You may also want to contact your state's equal opportunity department. While each state has such an entity, it has different names in different states. In New York, for example, it's the New York State Equal Opportunity Commission, while in Wyoming, it's the Department of Workforce Services.

ARBITRATION

If you are fired, and if you have a written employment contract or agreement, or if you have signed an arbitration agreement, a binding agreement signed by parties to a dispute when agreement is reached, usually with the help of a neutral arbitrator, you'll probably want to consult an attorney. He can help you determine the impact that document may have on the options available to you.

If you have signed an arbitration agreement—generally at the time you accepted a job offer—you've probably waived your right to sue under discrimination and/or other laws. Should you decide to pursue the case, you must then seek a resolution through arbitration.

Other contractual provisions may also alter, for better or for worse, the rights available to you as an employee. An attorney can work with you to take full advantage of your rights, as well as deal with complications arising from noncompete or other special provisions.

MEDIATION

In most at-will termination situations, employees have very little leverage to bring their employer to the negotiating table. In fact, mediation may work best if your employer believes that, unless he acquiesces to an alternative, he will be faced with litigation. Rather than deal with the time, bother, expense, and possible adverse publicity arising from a lawsuit, many employers would prefer to resolve a dispute out of court, even if they think the case against them may not be particularly strong.

At this juncture, you may choose to turn to your human resources department, employee assistance program, or, perhaps, your boss's boss for help in resolving your situation. Depending on your circumstances, on what you wish to accomplish, and on your employer, you may also want to consider seeking an outside mediator.

The key to the success of mediation, however, lies in the recognition by all parties of the need to reach a mutually acceptable agreement. If the will to do this does not exist, the mediation process will most likely fail. To put it simply, if you and your bully are facing each other across the negotiating table, mediation probably won't work.

In fact, if the decision whether to go to mediation is made by your bully, chances are you'll never even make it to the negotiating table. If he recognized the need to reach a mutually acceptable agreement, he wouldn't be a bully in the first place. However, if his boss is sitting across from you, your chances may be appreciably better.

Assuming that you choose mediation and your company agrees to go along, you won't have any problem locating mediators. However, finding one with whom both parties are comfortable may be more difficult.

You can probably find a nonprofit community mediation center that offers quality services to handle workplace disputes either at no charge or relatively inexpensively. The National Association for Community Mediation (www.nafcm.org) is a good place to start. Private-dispute resolution companies are more expensive, often charging $200 or more per hour, but still offering services at a cost considerably less than that typically involved in bringing a lawsuit.

In a dispute of this nature, mediation is most likely to involve an agent of the employer, the bully, and you. Unlike litigation, it is not intended as an adversarial proceeding, but rather to achieve the joint needs of all parties, enabling the disputants to work out their own solution. In short, it leaves open the possibility that you will be able to continue your employment.

Mediation is intended to focus less on assigning a monetary value to an issue, and more on redressing the inequities. Possible outcomes of mediation include apologies and promises of help in attaining another job, reinstatement to your job, or giving you an unjustly withheld promotion. Your bully could be transferred, fired, or required to undergo training. Or nothing at all may result.

When mediation succeeds, both sides benefit from a process that is typically quicker, less expensive and more private than litigation. An added incentive for the employer to go this route is that it is generally less disruptive to the workplace than a trial because the process is confidential and does not require witnesses. Finally, mediation promises less stress than litigation for all parties involved.

Alternately, you might want to turn to arbitration under the National Rules for the Resolution of Employment Disputes, a framework for conducting arbitration developed by the American Arbitration Association. You don't need an attorney on your side of the table, but the American Arbitration Association recommends you have one. You can find more about these rules and about the American Arbitration Association at www.adr.org.

But even if these options are available, they are no guarantees of success. Management and the human resources department may not really care or, if they do care, they might not take action.

PREPARING FOR MEDIATION

If you are contemplating mediation, you should follow the same steps as those for any legal proceeding. That includes making certain to keep all notes, email, and memos that you receive from the bully. If you receive verbal directions or criticism from him, write them down, request clarification or confirmation and return them, while keeping a copy for your records (See Chapter 5, "Your Options.").

In addition, take the time to clarify for yourself the resolution you are seeking, including the points that are most important to you as well as those that are least relevant. In other words, know what you want well before your first mediation session begins and develop a strategy that will help you to get it.

For more information, you might want to talk to a local mediation association or consult the National Association for Community Mediation at www.nafcm.org/pg1.cfm.

TAKING TIME OFF FROM WORK

Another option you may have in dealing with your bully is to take time off from work. Whether you take vacation, sick time, a sabbatical, or leave of absence, you'll have an opportunity to assess your options as well as gather your resources. You may ultimately decide to return from your leave and try to resolve your situation, or you may use your leave as a springboard for your departure.

In either case, make sure that you have all your legal ducks in a row. Inform your employer of your intention to take leave, and make sure that your leave is approved. Without such approval, you can be accused of having "abandoned" your job. If you're entitled to such leave, and your employer refuses to approve it, he's in violation of the law. This would give you credible grounds for a lawsuit.

AN EXAMPLE OF CONSTRUCTIVE
DISCHARGE: ARIZONA

The following is an excerpt from Arizona's constructive discharge statute:

*In any action under the statutes of this state (Arizona) or under
common law, constructive discharge may only be established by one of
the following:*

*1. Evidence of working conditions so difficult or unpleasant
that a reasonable employee would feel compelled to resign.
For constructive discharge to occur, the employee must give
the employer at least fifteen days' notice that the employee
intends to resign because of these conditions and that the
employer has failed to respond to the employee's concerns.*

*2. Evidence of "outrageous conduct" by the employer or his
agent that would cause a reasonable employee to feel compelled to resign. Such conduct might include sexual assault,
threats of violence directed at the employee, a continuous
pattern of discriminatory harassment by the employer or by
the employer's agent, or other similar conduct.*

If you have been with your employer for at least a year, look
into your eligibility for unpaid leave under the Family and Medical
Leave Act (FMLA). In addition to this federal law, many states have
comparable, and sometimes more generous, legislation with
regard to unpaid leave.

FAMILY AND MEDICAL LEAVE ACT

The Family and Medical Leave Act of 1993 entitles a covered employee to take up to 12 weeks of leave in a 12-month period for the birth
or adoption of a child, or to attend to the "serious health condition"
of the employee or the employee's child, spouse, or parent.

To protect this right, the FMLA prohibits your employer from
interfering with your ability to take this leave or retaliating against
you for opposing practices that the FMLA prohibits. If your
employer engages in these activities, the FMLA enables you to
bring suit for damages. Along these same lines, your employer may

Susan Futterman

not retaliate against you by firing you, either while you are on leave or after your return, for having taken leave under the FMLA. However, if you are fired while on leave or upon your return, you will need to establish that your employment was not terminated for some other, legally valid reason.

The Family and Medical Leave Act protects employees who have worked for a covered employer for at least 12 months and for at least 1,250 hours during the previous 12-month period. (The FMLA defines a covered employer as any person engaged in commerce—or in any industry or activity affecting commerce who employs 50 or more employees for each working day—during each of 20 or more calendar workweeks in the current or preceding calendar year.) If you are eligible for leave under FMLA and choose to take it, you are entitled to continue your employer-paid health benefits while on leave. If you work for a company not covered under the FMLA, check with your state labor department to see if your state has any comparable legislation.

SHORT-TERM DISABILITY

A few states, including California, Hawaii, New Jersey, New York, and Rhode Island, make short-term disability insurance (SDI) available to workers. Eligibility requirements vary from state to state, so make certain you know what the rules are before taking any action. In most cases, if work is deemed to be the sole or, in some cases, primary cause of your disability, you may not be eligible for short-term disability.

However, you may still be eligible if your doctor determines that your employment has aggravated an existing condition. In either case, if you are planning to file for other government programs including workers' compensation or Social Security, make sure your SDI diagnosis does not later interfere with your eligibility for a longer-term program.

If your boss continues to harass you while you are on disability, get in touch with an attorney. Your manager is violating the law and needs to stop. Don't forget to document such activity, since it may well provide you with additional leverage in negotiating a termination agreement or pursuing litigation. Similarly, on your return to

KELLIE'S STORY

I worked in the West Coast branch of a large, highly regarded law firm with offices all across the US. Everyone, from top management on down, including local human resource personnel, knew of my boss's pugnacious character.

As his assistant, day in and day out, I was the individual most often in the line of fire. His violence toward me escalated during the months I worked for him to the point where his tirades about my imagined incompetence were almost a daily occurrence. Going to work was like entering a war zone.

The last few months I was on the job, in order to provide myself with a modicum of job protection, I purposefully let a few coworkers know that if I were fired, I would fight the firm. I added that I had kept a very detailed diary of incidents, which wasn't true. I knew this information would make its way back to human resources with the speed of light. That I needed to leave my job was clear and I was laying the groundwork to depart on the strongest terms possible. I wanted to choose when I left, and on what terms. I did not want to be fired. I fought with the only thing left to fight with, the knowledge that this firm would do anything to avoid an employee lawsuit and/or bad publicity.

This tactic worked for me because the firm had heard in advance of my departure that I was considering a lawsuit. They knew their position was indefensible. Had it been a less clear-cut case of blatant harassment and employee abuse, the tactic would not have worked as well as it did. Providing me with a severance package was a far, far less expensive option than a lawsuit, which would have mired them in negative publicity for months, if not years, to come, in either local or national media. I motivated the firm to treat me fairly, and they did so.

To my mind, the biggest trump card for any employee of a large, well-known company is the company's fear of bad publicity. I know my firm was extremely concerned about that prospect and, as a consequence, I negotiated a decent severance package, something that they would never offer to anyone working at my level (administrative assistant to a senior partner). So, there are "ways" if you don't want to or have no legal grounds to sue to gain some recompense for your poor treatment. Play on their fear, as they played on yours the entire time you were their employee.

work following leave under FMLA, your employer must return you to your original job or to an equivalent job, with equivalent pay, benefits and working conditions. If he does not, he's breaking the law.

BREACH OF CONTRACT

If you are a union worker, professional athlete, a member of senior management, or an independent contractor, you are probably working under the terms of a contract. If you are abiding by the terms of that contract, your employer typically can't terminate you without good cause. However, if your contract includes an "escape clause" specifying that either party may unilaterally end the relationship without consequence, you are vulnerable to being "let go" with or without cause.

In some states, if employers don't explicitly document the terms of employment at will, the conditions of employment may, in some circumstances, be modified by provisions contained in employers' policy manuals, employee handbooks, employee agreements, and similar documents. Even if there is no formal modification made to your "at-will" employment, there may be factors that negate your employment at-will terms. Such factors include verbal assurances of job security and superior performance reviews.

But don't jump to the conclusion that you are not an at-will employee. Because your employer may well have taken precautions to protect itself from unintentionally negating that status, you'll want an expert opinion before making any assumptions. Similarly, even if such factors are present, you are probably out of luck if you signed an employment agreement that included a provision stating that such factors do not constitute a guarantee of continued employment. Under such a circumstance, your boss probably does not need a good reason to fire you.

DISCRIMINATION

As discussed earlier, under federal legislation, including Title VII, ADA, and ADEA, an employer cannot fire you solely on the basis of gender, race, creed, age, disability, national origin, and other specific factors.

Nevertheless, says attorney Paul Buchanan, a lot of the lawsuits that reach trial, while framed as discrimination issues, are really much less about discrimination, and much more about managers' lack of interpersonal skills. [1]

Whether those lawsuits are dismissed on summary judgment, tried in court, or settled out of court depends less on their merits than on the skill and creativity of the lawyers on either side. Although an unclear discrimination case is difficult to prove, defense attorneys typically try to keep such cases away from a jury, instead seeking a summary judgment or settlement negotiation. They are concerned that the jury's sympathy will be with the plaintiff even though the letter of the law may be on their side.

As the number of employment-related lawsuits continues to increase, some observers contend that employment litigation has posed a severe enough threat, has cost enough money, and attracted enough negative publicity that businesses are starting to respond by eliminating or retraining poor or abusive managers. Presumably, the prospect of new legislation that would make "equal opportunity" bullying illegal is also having an impact (See Chapter 17, "Legal Directions.").

Moreover, Buchanan notes, the courts are spurring both employee and employer to be more proactive at attempting to work out solutions before bringing cases to court. In fact, if the employer can show that the employee has not made a good-faith effort to resolve the issue with the employer, the latter may be able to persuade a judge to summarily dismiss the case.

Although larger companies tend to be held to higher standards, problems in smaller companies actually may be more severe. This is because in smaller companies the limelight is not so bright, and management layers, HR staff, and internal grievances processes usually do not exist.

UNEMPLOYMENT BENEFITS

In most instances, if you've been terminated from your job, you are entitled to collect unemployment benefits. Intended to provide financial assistance to eligible workers who are unemployed and who meet certain state eligibility requirements, unemployment benefits are administered separately by each state under guidelines established by federal law. Generally capped at a fraction of your take-home pay, unemployment benefits in most states are funded solely through a tax imposed on employers. That's another way of saying, your bully is paying for it. You've earned it. Take advantage of it.

CONSTRUCTIVE DISCHARGE DEFINED

If you, a reasonable person, have no option but to resign from your job, your resignation may qualify as a "constructive discharge" on the part of your employer. In other words, for all intents and purposes, you were fired.

Suppose that, rather than terminate your employment, your employer makes your continued presence in the workplace so intolerable that, rather than wait for him to say "you're fired," you submit your resignation—even just stop showing up for work. Your employer may nevertheless bear the same liability toward you, including payment of lost earnings and extension of certain benefits, as if he had expressly terminated your employment.

Spero points to five factors that the courts have found helpful in determining whether coercion or duress exists:

1. whether the employee was given some alternative to resignation

2. whether the employee understood the nature of the choice he was given

3. whether the employee was given a reasonable time in which to choose

4. whether the employee was permitted to select the effective date of the resignation

5. whether the employee had the advice of counsel

In order to qualify for unemployment, you must meet state requirements for wages earned or time worked during a specified baseline period. In addition, your unemployment must be determined to be through no fault of your own and you must meet other eligibility requirements of state law. As a consequence, under most circumstances, if you resign from your job, you are not eligible for unemployment benefits. However, there's an important exception to this rule. If your resignation is considered a constructive discharge, then you should be eligible for unemployment benefits. If you think you may be eligible, apply for these benefits. You've earned them. But don't expect too much—you'll only receive a fraction of your former compensation.

To file a claim, contact your state's unemployment insurance agency as soon as possible after becoming unemployed. In some states, you can now file a claim by telephone and/or via the Internet.

You may have a two- to three-week wait after filing your claim before you receive your first benefit check. In some states, that process takes even longer—you may need to wait six or more weeks to receive your first unemployment check. Most states will reject or delay your claim if you provide inaccurate or incomplete information. Be sure to obtain an application for benefits as soon as possible, and fill it out completely and accurately.

To continue receiving unemployment benefits, you must file periodic—weekly or biweekly—claims and respond to questions concerning your continued eligibility. In addition, you must report any earnings from work you had during the week(s). You must also report any job offers or work that you decline to do.

If you are denied benefits, you do have the right to file an appeal. Deadlines to file an appeal differ from state to state, so check with your unemployment office for the local deadline as well as for other information about your right to appeal. Your former employer also may dispute your unemployment benefits if he disagrees with the state's determination regarding your eligibility.

Your benefits will typically be based on a percentage of your earnings over a recent 52-week period, up to a stated maximum amount. Benefits usually are paid for a maximum of 26 weeks but can be extended during periods of high unemployment. Many states also offer, and sometimes require, participation in career workshops and training programs.

Benefits are subject to federal income taxes and must be reported on your federal income tax return. For more information, see www.workforcesecurity.doleta.gov/unemploy/uifactsheet.asp.

Whether you resigned your position or were fired, congratulations! You've gotten away from your bully and out of a toxic environment. You're ready to begin again.

FIVE STEPS TO CHOOSING A MEDIATOR

1. decide what you want from mediation:

· consider the level of intervention both parties want and will accept from a mediator

· think about the dispute and the framework in which you'd like to resolve it

2. based on feedback from all parties, develop a list of mediators—sources include:

· word of mouth

· yellow pages

· referral services, including www.mediate.com, your state bar association, and professional associations such as the Oregon Mediation Association, the Southern California Mediation Association, or the National Association for Community Mediation

3. assess the mediator's:

· training

· knowledge

· experience

4. interview mediators with regard to:

· ethics

· confidentiality

· logistics

· cost

5. evaluate information and make a decision

11.

WORKERS' COMPENSATION

Filing a workers' compensation claim is a good deal more difficult than those attorneys on late-night TV make it out to be. Claims related to stress-related disorders such as anxiety, post-traumatic stress disorder, and depression are almost always harder to prove than claims of physical injury. Moreover, they open up your life to a series of invasions by doctors, lawyers, and employers. If you're not willing and able to deal with all of this, you may be well-advised not to pursue a workers' compensation claim. Before you decide one way or another, make sure that you understand all of the pros and cons and that you have explored all of your options.

While workers' compensation has been compared to "no-fault" insurance, it is scarcely that. Stress-related workers' compensation claims, in particular, are difficult to substantiate and may well serve primarily to exacerbate the victim's difficulties. This means that, if you decide to file a workers' compensation complaint, you will almost certainly want to hire an attorney. In the US, most, if not all, attorneys specializing in workers' compensation work on contingency. That means that your attorney will receive a portion of the sum awarded to you by the court if you win your case or a percentage of the amount negotiated as a settlement, but will not otherwise receive a fee. You will, however, still be required to pay for upfront legal expenses that you or your attorney incur on your case (See Chapter 9, "Your Day in Court?".).

The attorney will evaluate the information you have gathered and help you decide if you have a winnable case under your state's law. However, even if you are persuaded that filing a claim is the right thing to do, the attorney won't take your case unless he thinks you have a good chance of winning, or at least reaching a substantial out-of-court settlement.

In a workers' compensation case regarding bullying, you will likely be claiming some sort of psychological or stress-related disability, perhaps with some associated physical symptoms, based on the treatment you received. So begin documenting any health-related issues with your doctor and/or therapist as early in the process as possible. You may be well-advised to seek out a specialist, a psychiatrist with experience dealing with stress-related disorders, and/or victims of emotional abuse.

In most cases, successful stress-related claims typically involve more tangible traumas than bullying such as an armed robbery, an act of workplace violence, a serious accident, or severe depression following a serious physical injury. (In the last instance, such a claim would probably not stand alone, but would supplement a physical injury case.)

KAREN: LOOKING ON THE BRIGHT SIDE

Whilst I look forward to [a] new career, I leave behind nearly 20 years of health-service experience and know I'm about to go to the bottom of the career ladder. But I accept this if it means I escape a situation that made me so ill.

If you, your doctor, and your attorney all agree that you should pursue a workers' compensation claim, you'll once again need to pull out all of your documentation. Gather the records of all of your symptoms and problems, descriptions of all the abusive behavior to which you've been subjected, your efforts to resolve your problems at work, the outcome of those efforts, and any other information your attorney deems pertinent.

A stress-related workers' comp claim will begin with close scrutiny into your psychological and emotional health, past, and present. Psychiatrists, at least some of them chosen by your employer and not necessarily impartial, will test and evaluate you.

In pursuing a workers' compensation claim, you can expect questions about virtually every aspect of your life. While your employer typically is not privy to the specifics, the insurance company is permitted to look into every possible stress factor that might have a bearing on your current mental condition, including, but not limited to financial information, deaths and illnesses in the family, marital problems, family problems, sexual problems, prior medical problems, substance-abuse issues, and past treatment for depression and anxiety. So by filing a workers' compensation claim, you are opening your life, past and present, up for examination by the defendants. Before you go down this path, make certain that this is something you really want to do, something that is worth all of the time, expense, and effort that this step will entail.

You should be prepared for the employer-retained psychiatrist to reject your claim. You and your attorney must be unfazed by that, and ready to counter with an expert opinion of your own, preferably from a psychiatrist who has courtroom experience and is accustomed to testifying.

In addition, your attorney should know exactly what he needs from the psychiatrist to argue your case successfully, and be willing to work closely with you and your doctor to ensure there will be no surprises during what could be a lengthy process.

IF YOUR CLAIM SUCCEEDS

Depending on your circumstances, your workers' compensation payment may come from a federal or state workers' compensation agency, your employer, or an insurance company acting on behalf of your employer. Workers' compensation eligibility and provisions vary according to who provides it. Federal workers are covered under the Federal Employees' Compensation Act (FECA), which is administered by the Office of Workers' Compensation Programs (OWCP). Workers injured while employed by private companies or by state and local government agencies are covered under state law, which varies from state to state.

If you have filed a workers' compensation claim, you cannot be terminated because of your inability to perform required tasks (See Chapter 9, "Your Day in Court?".). Thus, you may have a solid wrongful termination case if you filed a workers' compensation claim and then were fired, whether for inability to do your job or in retaliation for filing a claim.

However, if you cannot adequately fulfill your job functions because of your disability, your employer may be entitled to suspend your pay to you until such time as you are able to satisfy all of the requirements of your job. If you are able to do all that is required in your position, but for some reason choose not to fulfill your job functions, your employer may have legitimate grounds to terminate your employment.

REACHING AN ACCOMMODATION

"The interactive process requires communication and good-faith exploration of possible accommodations between employers and individual employees. The shared goal is to identify an accommodation that allows the employee to perform the job effectively. Both sides must communicate directly, exchange essential information and neither side can delay or obstruct the process."
—*from Ninth Circuit Court of Appeals in* Barnett v. US Air, Inc.

Keep in mind, however, that all you're obligated to do is meet your job requirements. Moreover, under the Americans with Disabilities Act, your employer may be required to offer you an "accommodation" to enable you to do your job effectively. Perhaps the most common accommodation in workers' compensation cases involving verbal abuse in the workplace is a transfer away from your bully. However, if the company you work for is small, such an accommodation may not be feasible.

WORKERS' COMPENSATION AND
SOCIAL SECURITY

Okay, now the confusing stuff. Ordinarily, disability payments from other sources do not affect Social Security disability benefits. But, of course, nothing is that simple. If your disability payment comes from a public disability program such as workers' compensation, your Social Security benefits will be reduced. The combined amount of your Social Security benefit and your public disability payment cannot exceed 80 percent of your average earnings when you were last on the job.

However, while you won't receive the total benefit amount,

you may need to report the total from both programs for income tax purposes.

OTHER PUBLIC DISABILITY PAYMENTS

Unlike workers' compensation benefits, which are paid only for job-related disabilities, payments from other public disability programs do not have to be related to a disability incurred at work. As noted above, they may affect any payments you receive from Social Security.

Civil service disability benefits, military disability benefits, state temporary disability benefits, and state or local government retirement benefits that are based on disability all fit into this category. For more information on how these and other programs may affect your Social Security benefits, check with your local Social Security office, or online at www.ssa.gov/pubs/10018.html.

WHILE YOU'RE AWAY

Although you may not be terminated from your job because you are out on workers' compensation leave, you can be terminated from your job even though you are out on workers' compensation. That is, if your employer is already laying people off and you just happened to be on workers' compensation leave at the time, you can be cut along with the others. However, if you choose to file a suit claiming that your termination was retaliatory in nature, your employer would be required to establish that your discharge was unrelated to your workers' compensation claim.

Similarly, if an employer claims to fire you for poor performance but you believe that it was illegal, you would have to prove that the motive underlying the firing was illegal. In other words, you would need to establish that your termination stemmed, at least in part, from the fact that you filed a workers' compensation claim.

Remember that your employer only has a limited right to medical information directly related to your workers' compensation claim. The Health Insurance Portability and Accountability Act (HIPAA) of 1996 privacy rules allow a covered entity (such as a healthcare provider) to disclose protected health information if needed to comply with workers' compensation laws, but does not specify when such a disclosure is required. Your lawyer should be keeping a close eye, not only on the latest HIPAA regulations, but on the privacy of your medical history as a whole.

LAURA'S STORY

Any way you look at it, though, a stress-related workers' compensation claim is not an easy road to follow. Finding a lawyer was probably the most stressful part. At first, I kept searching for a workers' compensation lawyer and none of them wanted to take a "stress claim" without physical injuries and an underlying neurological condition.

I lost count of how many of them I contacted. The first one willing was such a sleazeball from the first sight that I walked away. The second one was nice, but we both agreed that my first priority would be securing a transfer, so I needed a lawyer specializing in employment and/or disability accommodations.

All disability lawyers I contacted were asking first if I was using a wheelchair. When I said "no," that was usually the end of the conversation. The most abrupt lawyers were those who had physical disabilities themselves (I was referred to a couple of physically handicapped lawyers as the "potentially most compassionate ones." This was the wrong assumption). Some didn't even bother to return my calls after I left upfront messages telling them that my handicap is "invisible," meaning that I'm not mobility-impaired, blind, or deaf.

Workers' compensation laws vary from state to state. In most states, employers generally have the right only to information regarding employees' functional limitations that may affect job performance. Check with your state labor department to see what information will be available to prospective employers if you file a workers' compensation claim with your current employer.

WORKING WITH A DISABILITY

If your physician places you on disability for symptoms such as severe depression, anxiety, or panic attacks, he can also specify that your employer must accommodate any special needs that arise out of your disability when you return to work. Under the law, the employer is required to provide "reasonable accommodation," as explained by the Equal Employment Opportunity Commission. Reasonable accommodation generally can be characterized as "any change in the work environment or in the way things are customarily done that enables an individual with a disability to enjoy equal employment opportunities."[1]

When you return to work, the doctor will need to provide your employer with the specifics of what tasks you can and cannot perform. However, the employer is not entitled to any portion of your medical records or to any details of your diagnosis without your explicit permission. And there is no reason for you to provide such permission.

Returning to work with an accommodation request may be a means for you to obtain a transfer away from your bully. However, that strategy works best with larger companies. If the firm is small, there simply may be no place for you to go. Moreover, your employer does not have to meet your accommodation request if he can establish that accommodating your disability represents a hardship for the company.

Keep in mind, too, that if you request an accommodation, the company again has the right to have you examined by a doctor of its choice.

AFTER A WORKERS' COMPENSATION CLAIM

Whether your workers' compensation claim proved successful or not, it could come back to haunt you during your search for a new job. In some states, it is legal for companies with 15 or more employees to review workers' compensation records after a conditional job offer has been made. The law in your state also may allow those companies to review your medical history after a conditional job offer has been extended. In no state is it legal for a prospective employer to review those records before such an offer has been made.

Although the information available is generally limited to determining whether the subject of the investigation has filed a claim, some states, such as Colorado, Florida, Illinois, and Ohio consider workers' compensation files to be public records. Other states will not release any information. Check with your state's labor department to find out where you stand.

12.

PROTECTING YOUR HEALTH

By the time you've hit your thirties, you've probably collected a medical condition that insurers will deem to be a "pre-existing condition," be it a bad knee, asthma, low thyroid, or hay fever. The sad truth is, you're stuck with it. And that you may have a difficult time finding an insurer who's willing to issue you a policy unless you've made the appropriate plans.

That's a particularly difficult position to be in, especially, if you're out of work, or about to be. Yet, if you don't have a job, protecting your health is more important than ever.

HEALTH INSURANCE

Insurance is not a particularly pleasant topic, even when you aren't under financial pressure. When you are facing financial pressure, it can be downright grim. But that doesn't make having the right insurance, particularly healthcare coverage, any less essential. If you have had health coverage as an employee benefit and you leave your job, voluntarily or otherwise, one of your first concerns will be maintaining protection against the ever-rising cost of healthcare.

As always, if you are able to plan ahead, so much the better. Most likely, however you will still have some loose ends to tie up and some decisions to make when you leave your job.

If you're still at work, review your benefits. If you have a Healthcare Reimbursement Account (HCRA) or Flexible Spending Account (FSA)—in which a portion of your salary is set aside tax-free to use for reimbursement of qualified medical expenses—make sure you use it before you leave. If you don't, you'll lose the contributions you've made, counsels Dori Miller, a health care insurance specialist at Smith & Crakes, Inc.

Even more important, make sure you have adequate health insurance coverage after your job ends. Depending on your situation, you may have a number of options. If you are moving from one employer to another, you can, of course, expect to obtain coverage from your new employer. If you and your family are already covered by your spouse's insurance policy, then you don't have to do a thing. However, if neither of these situations apply, you have some decisions to make.

COBRA

If you work for a company with 20 or more employees, you are almost certainly eligible for insurance coverage once you leave. Under COBRA, employers must offer a former employee the option of continuing coverage under the company's group health insurance plan at the worker's own expense for some time after employment ends. Employees also have the option of including their families on a COBRA policy.

In general, COBRA gives an employee who quits or is dismissed for reasons other than gross misconduct the right to continue group health coverage for 18 months. In some other circumstances, such as the death of the employee, that employee's dependents can continue coverage for up to 36 months. In virtually all cases, this coverage is significantly more expensive then it is for still-current employees, but is probably significantly less expensive than comparable coverage purchased individually.

If your employer does not come under COBRA's mandate, you still may be covered by a state program. A number of states extend coverage similar to COBRA to workers in firms with two or more employees. In California, for example, Cal-COBRA provides equivalent benefits for employees of small companies.

Your employer and/or the insurance carrier are required by law to inform you of your coverage under the federal COBRA program or a state equivalent. (Your COBRA insurance plan administrator should send you information and instructions within 44 days of your departure.) But don't wait for either of them to provide you with the information you need. Call your old office manager, human resources department, or the insurance company itself, and ask for it. If you don't receive the necessary forms and information promptly, repeat your request, this time in writing.

In states that mandate COBRA-like coverage for small group health plans, continuing access to benefits must be offered to any qualified beneficiary who would lose coverage under the plan as a result of termination, and who elects in writing to continue coverage within a specified timeframe. Your former employer is obligated to work with its health insurance carrier to ensure that you are properly notified of your right to continue your benefits.

Complicating your task—but possibly improving your coverage—is the Health Insurance Portability and Accountability Act of 1996, which has significantly expanded the protections available to many Americans.

HIPAA HOORAY

Among other impacts, HIPAA generally restricts the ability of insurers to refuse you coverage based on a pre-existing condition, but only if you have fully exhausted your COBRA coverage before applying for a new policy. Pre-existing conditions include serious health problems such as heart ailments, diabetes, and cancer, as well as relatively minor, common ailments such as allergies.

As a consequence of HIPAA's restrictions, if you or a member of your family has a pre-existing condition, you should seriously consider electing and exhausting your coverage under COBRA before obtaining new insurance.

Your efforts to obtain a new policy may, in any case, be moot. If you, like many of the bullied, are seeing a psychologist, a psychiatrist, or any sort of therapist for issues arising from your work, an insurer will most likely be able to deny you conventional insurance coverage.

If pre-existing conditions aren't an issue, then you may choose to forgo COBRA and save money on health insurance. However, according to the US Department of Health and Human Resources, if you decline COBRA coverage, you subsequently will not be covered by HIPAA unless and until the cycle starts all over again, i.e., you obtain coverage under a qualifying policy.

Although HIPAA does not eliminate all use of pre-existing condition exclusions, it does limit those that can be imposed. In addition, it expands the circumstances under which you may be able to extend your coverage after the initial 18-month COBRA period has expired.

Even though HIPAA's role begins as soon as you leave your job, you will not feel its impact until after your COBRA coverage ends. In addition to limiting the exclusions that insurers can impose for pre-existing conditions, HIPAA prohibits group health plans from denying coverage or charging extra for coverage based on your or your family member's past or present poor health, and may also guarantee you the right to purchase health insurance.

If you're currently in treatment, are planning to have surgery or taking expensive medication, you'll probably want to use COBRA to remain covered through your current plan. If you do not extend your coverage under COBRA, you could find out, after it's too late, that you are not eligible for conventional health insurance.

In short, HIPAA may reduce your prospects of losing existing coverage, make it easier to switch health plans, and/or help you buy coverage on your own if you lose your employer's plan and have no other coverage available. If you're eligible for HIPAA, you are eligible to receive individual coverage.

Although HIPAA is designed to help guarantee your future insurability, it unfortunately does not apply in all circumstances. Once you disclose a medical condition to your insurance company, that condition is on your record.

HIPAA, as discussed earlier, will only protect insurability if you first exhaust your COBRA continuation coverage, which typically lasts 18 months. If you chose to apply for disability payments during that period, your participation in COBRA would not change, and you could continue to exercise whatever remains of your 18 months of coverage. However, if you terminate your coverage before exhausting COBRA coverage, you'll lose your HIPAA protection. And, due to your disability, you would almost certainly be denied coverage in the non-group or individual market.

In other words, if you qualify for disability, you will not qualify for underwritten insurance in the open market. However, if you continue to pay for your COBRA coverage and ultimately exhaust that coverage, you'll be in significantly better shape. With your COBRA coverage exhausted, HIPAA guarantees you eligibility for individual insurance coverage. You cannot be turned down for insurance under this program even if you are receiving disability benefits.

In short, although expensive, continuing to pay your premiums for COBRA coverage will likely prove worthwhile. To obtain individual coverage as a HIPAA-eligible individual, you must have opted for and exhausted COBRA continuation coverage if that coverage was available to you. In addition, you will not be considered HIPAA-eligible if your prior coverage was cancelled because you did not pay your premiums or committed fraud, and/or if you are eligible for Medicare or Medicaid. You may also have to satisfy other requirements to obtain the coverage. Check with your state insurance department for up-to-date and specific information.

To make sure your window of opportunity doesn't slam shut, start looking for new insurance before your COBRA coverage is exhausted. You only have two months following the end of your COBRA eligibility to get new insurance. By starting early, you can ensure that you have seamless coverage.

A month or two before your COBRA benefits end, contact your state's insurance department and ask how a person eligible for individual insurance under HIPAA goes about getting insurance. An easy way to find your state's insurance department is to log on to the National Association of Insurance Commissioners (NAIC) Web site at www.naic.org.

You'll likely need proof of COBRA insurance coverage to qualify for HIPAA continuation. If your ex-employer doesn't send proof—as he is required to do—by the time your COBRA insurance coverage is nearing its end, contact the company or your plan administrator.

For more information, see the US Department of Labor's Web site at www.dol.gov/dol/topic/health-plans/portability.htm and contact your state insurance commissioner's office for details about HIPAA-like coverage that may be available on a state level. Health insurance companies that offer individual plans also may provide HIPAA information.

Depending on your financial situation and health status, you may also be eligible for Medicaid, a federal program administered at the state level. A helpful overview of your insurance options is located on the US Health and Human Services Web site at www.ahrq.gov/consumer/insuranc.htm.

HIGH-RISK HEALTH INSURANCE POOLS

A high-risk health insurance pool is one you don't want to jump into unless you have to. It's a last resort for those who have been denied traditional insurance because of health problems, such as cancer, stroke, chronic depression, or heart disease.

If you have a break in your insurance and have gone without insurance for a specified period, usually about two months, a pre-existing condition clause can be imposed. Any condition for which you've been treated—usually within the past six months, but possibly for a longer period—will be held against you. That may mean that a health insurance risk pool is your best, if not your only, bet.

Health insurance risk pools are special programs created by state legislatures to provide coverage for individuals who may otherwise be uninsurable. Although the health benefits vary, most are comparable to basic private market plans except for cost. Typically, pools charge between 130 percent and 200 percent above the standard premium for individual health insurance on the open market.

Despite the expense, you might find yourself on a waiting list to get into a state insurance pool. This is because the only other alternative for many people with costly medical conditions is to go uninsured.

Most high-risk health insurance pools have strict eligibility guidelines, so not everyone who has a serious illness qualifies for coverage. You can't apply for health insurance through a high-risk pool if you're eligible for assistance from any other state or federal program such as COBRA, Medicaid, or Medicare.

There is one exception to mandatory waiting periods. Under federal law, if you're eligible for the risk pool and have had continuous health insurance coverage under a group policy without a lapse in coverage for more than 63 days, you can receive coverage immediately.

GET IT IN WRITING

Whenever you leave any health plan, either group or individual, you should obtain a "certificate of creditable coverage" in writing from your insurance carrier. Your certificate should include:

- your coverage dates
- your policy ID number
- the insurer's name and address
- any family members included under your coverage

You also can use other evidence to prove creditable coverage, including:

- pay stubs that reflect a health insurance premium deduction
- explanation-of-benefit forms
- a benefit-termination notice from Medicare or Medicaid
- verification letter from your doctor or your former health insurance provider confirming that you had prior coverage

To determine your creditable coverage, insurers can look at your coverage for five specific benefits: prescription medications, vision, dental, mental health, and substance abuse treatment. Most likely, the insurance carrier will send you the certificate of eligibility automatically, if more slowly, than you might like. Still, it never hurts to ask for a copy.

PERSONAL DISABILITY

Personal disability insurance is not nearly as common as health or life insurance. If you don't have it when you leave your job, you won't be able to get a policy. However, if you already have a policy, you may find that it pays off very nicely.

If you have purchased individual disability insurance, then your policy will likely replace anywhere from 45 percent to 60 percent of your gross income on a tax-free basis should your doctor diagnose you with a condition that prevents you from earning an income in your occupation. Payments under such a policy are tax-free.

You may also be covered under an employer-provided policy. If you're not sure whether you do have company-provided insurance, check with the HR department, office manager, or other appropriate individual at your workplace.

SYLVIA'S STORY

I wanted to file a workers' compensation claim to take three months' stress leave from my workplace, at the very least. I went to my doctor and discussed the situation with her. She had the workers' compensation forms in her office and filled one out for me, stating that I was enduring severe stress in a workplace situation. She wrote that I was going to have three months off with a review every month. My employer was my bully, and he stated that he was going to sue me and my doctor if I continued with my claim.

I did not go ahead with my workers' compensation application, and decided to take any sick days owing in a desperate attempt to get away from the nightmare for a short time. While I was off work, I decided to leave this organization as I knew that I could not change anything.... I don't regret it one bit.

Although her employer's threat effectively prevented Sylvia from taking action, it actually may have improved her legal standing. Had she decided to go forward with a workers' compensation claim, that threat would likely provide grounds for a lawsuit, even if it did not succeed.

If you pay the premiums for an individual disability policy, payments you receive under the policy are not subject to income tax. If your employer has paid some or all of the premiums under a group disability policy, some or all of the benefits may be taxable.

If you are still employed and considering disability income insurance, you will need to evaluate different policies. Here are some things to look for:

· Some policies pay benefits only if you are unable to perform the duties of your customary occupation, while others pay only if you can not work at all. Make sure that you know the insurer's definition of disability before you purchase a policy.

· Some policies pay only for accidents—far more useful are those that insure for illness as well. If you are shopping for a policy, make sure that the one you purchase covers both accident and illness.

· Benefits may begin anywhere from one month to six months or more after the onset of disability. A later starting date can mean lower premiums. At the same time, however, if your policy only starts to pay, for example, three months after the disability begins, you may lose a considerable amount of income.

· Benefits may be payable for a period ranging anywhere from one year to a lifetime. Since disability benefits replace income, most people only need benefits up to their planned retirement age. But it's generally wise to insure at least until age 65 since a lengthy disability threatens financial security much more than a short disability.

Finally, find out what you can about the insurer's track record on payment of claims. See if your state insurance department records the number of complaints each company receives (For a link to your state insurance department Web site, see the National Association of Insurance Commissioners' Web site at www.naic.org/state_contacts/sid_websites.htm.).

Even if you had private disability insurance when you left your job, you may have problems getting your insurer to pay the claim. In recent years, disability insurers have diminished in number. Those that have survived have confronted soaring claims and declining premiums and, in response, have become increasingly loath to pay on claims.

As a result, if you become injured and disabled, your policy benefits may be delayed or denied. In some cases, you may only receive benefits if you hire an attorney and file suit against your insurer, particularly if your claim involves a disability that is relatively difficult to establish, such as stress. Moreover, under the terms of the policy itself, benefits involving certain mental disorders or other conditions may be limited to two years.

If your policy defines total disability as "own-occupation disability," you'll probably have the best prospect of collecting. Under this definition, if you are disabled and cannot perform the principal duties of the job you currently have, you get paid your disability benefit even if you can do some other tasks.

READ THE FINE PRINT

Complicated to begin with, the rules and regulations surrounding health insurance change rapidly and sometimes dramatically. Before you make any commitment with regard to insurance that could affect your ability to obtain coverage in the future, be sure that all of your information is up to date and accurate. Before you make any decisions, consult an insurance professional and/or check with your state department of insurance.

The most conservative definition of total disability is "any-occupation disability." Under this definition, you do not receive any benefits unless you are completely unemployed and unable to do any work. Many companies, of course, will define "disability" in shades of gray between own-occupation and any-occupation disability. And some disability insurance products will give you own-occupation coverage for a specified period, then move you to a modified plan, increasingly contingent on whether you can produce any income.

OWN-OCCUPATION DISABILITY INSURANCE

This is the most comprehensive definition of total disability available. This type of policy will have a definition that says because of a covered sickness or accident you are unable to perform the material and substantial duties of your regular occupation. The insurer is obligated to pay the claim even if you are engaged in some other capacity in a different occupation.

Under this type of plan, the bottom line is that you will be considered totally disabled if you cannot perform in your occupation because of a sickness or injury.

INCOME-REPLACEMENT INSURANCE

This is the most common type of disability coverage. Most insurance carriers that have stopped offering own-occupation disability insurance have moved to income-replacement insurance.

Under a typical income-replacement policy, you will qualify only if, because of sickness or injury, you are unable to perform the material and substantial duties of your occupation, and are not engaged in any other occupation.

Thus, the income-replacement definition will penalize you during a claim if you make the decision to return to work, or earn another source of earned income while on a claim.

GAINFUL OCCUPATION INSURANCE

This is probably the most common employer-sponsored group long-term disability insurance policy and is the most limited form of disability insurance. Essentially, under gainful-occupation insurance, you are covered when, because of sickness or injury, you are unable to perform the material and substantial duties of your occupation, or any occupation for which you are deemed reasonably qualified by education, training, or experience. Thus you may not qualify for insurance payments if you are capable of doing a much-lower level job.

STATE DISABILITY INSURANCE

California, Hawaii, New Jersey, New York, Rhode Island, and Puerto Rico all offer disability benefits as part of their unemployment insurance programs. These state programs typically require applicants to submit their medical records as well as evidence that they had requested a leave of absence from their employer.

Employers may also provide additional disability coverage in these states as well as in the rest of the country. So, if you are unable to work, one of your first steps should be to inquire what insurance your employer provides. If you also have private disability coverage, you'll want to file a claim with that insurance carrier as well.

To determine whether your state offers such a disability program and whether you qualify, call your local unemployment insurance and workers' compensation insurance offices (See the US Department of Labor's Web site at www.dol.gov/esa/regs/compliance/owcp/wc.htm to obtain contact information for the appropriate agency in your state.).

In California, for example, you may be eligible for State Disability Insurance (SDI), a partial wage-replacement insurance plan. SDI is mandated by the state and funded through employee payroll deductions. SDI provides short-term benefits to eligible workers who suffer a loss of wages when they are unable to work due to an illness or injury, or a medically disabling condition from pregnancy or childbirth.

However if your work is deemed to be the sole cause of your disability, you may not be eligible for SDI. If, instead, work exacerbates an existing condition, you may be.

If your doctor deems your disability to be complete, you are under no obligation to provide your employer with any details of the diagnosis. Nevertheless, your employer may insist that you do so. He may be trying to intimidate you. Don't let him.

In most instances, workers' compensation requires that work-related disability constitute at least 51 percent of total disability. Thus, if you are eligible for SDI, you almost certainly will not be able to file for workers' compensation.

Although not all California employees are covered by SDI, approximately 12 million are. Administered by the California Employment Development Department (EDD), SDI coverage is not dependent on staying with a specific employer, and cannot be canceled or denied because of health risk factors, pre-existing medical conditions, or hazardous employment.

Should you take state disability leave, you may, in most cases, resign your position while still on SDI and continue to receive benefits for up to 52 weeks following a seven-day waiting period. However, if your employer terminates you prior to your doctor determining that you are fit to return to work, you may have grounds for a wrongful termination suit, particularly if your termination is in response to, or in retaliation of, your decision to take SDI leave (See Chapter 9, "Your Day in Court?".). Depending on the nature of your disability, the Americans with Disabilities Act may come into play.

Be aware that any legal action that involves stress-related injuries will likely give your employer some level of access to your medical data, both past and present. In addition, the emotional strain related to litigation may outweigh the possible benefits you may receive. Finally, debilitating stress caused by the workplace is a very difficult case to make.

NOT INCLUDED

The following payments do not count when deciding if your Social Security benefit will be reduced:

- Veterans Benefits Administration benefits
- federal benefits, if the work you did to earn them was covered by Social Security
- state and local government benefits, if the work you did to earn them was covered by Social Security
- private pensions or insurance benefits
- Supplemental Security Income (SSI) payments

If your disability coverage falls under the jurisdiction of the federal Employee Retirement Income Security Act (ERISA), you have the right to judicial review of the insurer's decision to deny benefits should the carrier refuse payment. If successful in court, you may force the insurer to pay the improperly denied benefits and may also recover attorneys' fees, but you probably won't be successful with a lawsuit for emotional distress or punitive damages.

SHORT-TERM DISABILITY

If your employer provides short-term disability, your coverage may only be available if you work more than 20 hours per week and you are off work for two consecutive weeks. You likely will not get paid during a two-week waiting period (you are expected to use sick or vacation time), and when you do get paid, the payments may be based on your years of employment.

Often, employer-paid short-term disability policies will limit you to a total of 24 weeks on short-term disability in any 12-month period. Monthly benefits are usually 60 percent of your income at the time of purchase, although cost-of-living adjustments may be available.

13.

LEAVING YOUR JOB

The good news is you're finally getting rid of your bully. The bad news is that you're going to have deal with him a little longer, until you get the details of your departure straightened out.

There are no two ways about it, leaving your job without another one waiting is stressful, whether you've quit or been fired. Nevertheless, if you don't take a deep breath, marshal your resources, and do what it takes to move forward, you're likely to regret it later.

As you extricate yourself from a toxic work environment, you're trying to achieve the best possible results for yourself while dealing with the damage your bully has inflicted. Don't expect the impossible of yourself.

If you decide you want to negotiate a termination agreement, but need help in making your exit, get it. It will pay off later. Even if your case never makes it to mediation, you may want to speak with a professional mediator, attorney, or therapist, someone who can help you develop the knowledge, tools, and resources you'll need to deal effectively with your employer.

If you can successfully confront your bully and negotiate a great settlement, wonderful. But if you can't, well, it's hardly surprising. If you find advice here that seems sound to you, and you simply can't deal with it right now, file it away for future reference. In the meantime, do the best you can and move on.

NEGOTIATING YOUR EXIT

Although some career counselors would have you focus on not rocking the boat any further, by following that advice you could be doing yourself a huge disservice. So forget about smiling bravely and making a graceful, unobtrusive exit. Instead, take a look at the possibility of obtaining a termination agreement from your employer. If you are able to negotiate one, figure out how to get the best deal for yourself that you can.

Think carefully about what you want and about what leverage you have available to get it. Do you have enough evidence to file a lawsuit, even if the odds are against you prevailing? If so, perhaps your company will deal a little more generously with you to avoid the expense, the exposure and the aggravation of going to court.

If you're pursuing a termination agreement, negotiating for the best references you can get should be near the top of your list. You want more than merely a verification of your employment dates and salary. Ideally, you'll write the letter of recommendation yourself and have your soon-to-be former employer sign it. This permits you the opportunity to make sure the right things are said about you. Be truthful but positive. This is not the time to be modest. Play up your strengths while minimizing or omitting your weaknesses. You may be surprised at what your soon-to-be ex-employer is willing to sign if it makes his life easier.

You may not get what you want. Your employer may refuse to provide a positive reference. In fact, furnishing any information that goes beyond your term of employment and other basic information may simply be against company policy. Still, it's worth a try.

In the same vein, your employer may want something from you. Perhaps, for example, he wants you to agree to a noncompete or nondisclosure clause as part of your termination agreement. If that's the case, make certain that you are receiving something you value in return, such as more severance pay or a positive letter of reference. Otherwise, you are simply doing your employer a favor without receiving anything for it. Speak with your attorney before you sign any of your rights away.

Would it be helpful to you to use your office, or at least your office voicemail and email in your job search? If so, request continued access for a period of weeks, or even months. Do you want to see if you can get your employer to pay an extra month's healthcare premiums? Ask. Also make sure you get all the benefits to which you are entitled, whether in the form of company stock, pension benefits, or medical coverage. The worst your employer can say is no. What else is he going to do, fire you?

Be careful about signing any waivers that will preclude you from pursuing legal action against the company. Depending on the nature of the severance package your about-to-be former employer offers, you may decide to waive your rights. That's fine. Just make sure your decision is an informed one.

GOVERNMENT BENEFIT PROGRAMS

· Unemployment Insurance: This program may provide some financial help if, through no fault of your own, you lose your job, temporarily or permanently.

· Workers' Compensation: If you cannot work because of a work-related injury or illness, and if you meet all of the requirements, workers' compensation is the program most likely to provide you with replacement income promptly. It may also pay the medical bills resulting from a workplace injury or illness, and/or compensate you for a permanent injury.

· Social Security Disability Insurance: This is intended to provide income to adults who, because of injury or illness, cannot work for at least 12 months. You may also be entitled to payments through a private disability insurance program if you were paying for it through payroll withholdings, or if your employer paid for such premiums (See Chapter 12, "Protecting Your Health.").

Once again, it's important to be realistic about what you can and cannot do. You may be in too much turmoil to be a very effective negotiator or even to cope with it at all. To expect yourself to deal with your employer head-on may be too much to ask right now. Talk over your options with someone you trust, and then decide how far to push, if you want to push at all.

Now that you're on your way out, it may be time for a second look at your legal options. If the harassment you faced was linked to a factor such as your age, your gender, your national origin, or your religion, you may have a case. If you were forced out or fired in retaliation for an action you took that is protected by law, you also may want to sue. Be aware that there's probably a time limit after which you'll no longer be able to file a suit (See Chapter 5, "Your Options," for help in reviewing your options, as well as the benefits and disadvantages of pursuing litigation.).

CAN YOUR EMPLOYER SUE YOU?

Your employer is entitled to sue you, just as you are entitled to sue your employer. The question is, of course, whether he can establish a valid legal claim. If you've absconded with proprietary secrets, breached a nondisclosure agreement, or violated a binding nocompete agreement or other legal contract, you may be prudent to consult a good attorney.

But what if a prospective candidate for your old position calls you for information on your old manager? You probably don't want to mislead that person into taking the same job that drove you up the wall. So the best course to take may be to do precisely what your former employer will likely do. Don't engage in hyperbole. Tell the truth in terms that are noncommittal, yet in ways that would raise flags for anyone who is listening carefully.

By definition, libel is a defamatory claim that is written. Slander is a defamatory claim that is spoken. To be defamatory, a statement must be false. However, although harsh comments may be completely accurate, you may be wise and would appear more professional if you erred on the side of discretion.

HANDLING THE EXIT INTERVIEW

Exit interviews, often held with employees who have been terminated as well as those who have voluntarily resigned, are frequently conducted for a variety of laudable reasons, such as helping the company to understand what it can do to improve retention and recognize and resolve problems in the workplace.

For you, the departing employee, they are fundamentally irrelevant. You don't have any obligation to help your soon-to-be former employer improve. But if you do care to share any information with the human resources department, do not do so while you are upset. Be very aware that one function of exit interviews is to guard against potential legal action and adverse publicity. You should also keep in mind that if you are contemplating any legal action against the company, you may be informing them of your moves by participating in the exit interview.

CINDY'S STORY

Last October, I collapsed at work after approximately five years of being bullied by a supervisor. The next day I went to my doctor who suggested I see a psychiatrist at the hospital to help me deal with what was going on. I did so and have been seeing her every four to six weeks. Meanwhile, she released me to return to work in February (prior to this I was being bullied and harassed long distance by letters from work and sheriffs' deputies coming to my door to deliver subpoenas and letters). I went back to work with an accommodation and after working part of the day was called into the commissioner's office and told by the personnel officer that my doctor's slip was not sufficient and I needed to see their doctor.

After receiving their doctor's approval, I went back to work. Evidently it still wasn't enough. Thereafter a sheriff's deputy and then the undersheriff showed up at our area to talk to me (two separate incidents) with finally the undersheriff threatening to arrest me for criminal trespassing if I didn't leave. I have been out of work ever since.

Finally, in many larger companies, your comments will probably become part of an anonymous body of information that never specifically mentions your manager. They're unlikely to have any direct impact on your former manager and/or coworkers. So what's the point?

Whether you have resigned from your job or have been fired, you are not required to answer any questions during an exit interview. If you do choose to answer the questions, do not agree to sign any notes that the human resources representative has made of the meeting. You could be waiving your rights to any future action against the company or inadvertently signing off on comments that don't accurately reflect your situation.

In short, as tempting as it may be to give HR the complete lowdown on your bullying boss, you would probably be wise to remain polite and noncommittal in your remarks or, better yet, skip the whole affair completely.

14.

REALITY STRIKES

"Success is not the key to happiness. Happiness is the key to success.
If you love what you are doing, you will be successful."
—*Albert Schweitzer*

It's done. It's your last day. You've brought in the packing boxes. Your spouse is parked outside waiting for you. You've packed away the last of your belongings and are getting ready to close the door on this particular chapter of your life.

You may feel relieved, perhaps a little numb, maybe just plain happy to be out. It may take awhile to sink in but whatever your mood is now, you can anticipate that at some point you will also feel some combination of sadness, anger, depression, failure, guilt, or even shame. This is all normal. The feelings are okay and necessary. You've gone through a tough experience, possibly a downright traumatic one. Whatever your feelings are, don't try to hide them from your family and friends, much less from yourself.

Before you go any further, take some time out if you can. Don't look at want ads. Don't check job sites on the Internet. Don't mass mail your resume or rush into anything. Instead, step back and get your bearings. Let yourself have some time to recover, relax, and enjoy yourself. Finances may be tight, but a few days to take care of yourself could prove priceless down the road. This may also be the ideal time to reassess your career path and see what changes, if any, are in order. Is the work you were doing the work you want to continue to do? Or can you see something else for yourself that would be more rewarding?

Find out how you really feel about what has been happening, now that you no longer have to maintain your defenses against your feelings. Spend some time with your family or friends or just with yourself.

Indulge your feelings. You're going to have to get back to being your mature, rational self soon enough. Just for once, give yourself a break. Don't minimize your experience. It was traumatic and hurtful and damaging. It may have inflicted damage on your health, your personal relationships, your finances, and your career. You have every right to be upset about it.

SIMON'S STORY

I quit on a Tuesday afternoon. I just couldn't take any more. I was depressed by the whole thing, but relieved that it was over. I figured if I just powered on through, I'd be fine. But I wasn't. I couldn't. I guess some people react by drinking or doing drugs. I reacted by sleeping. For a couple of days, I barely got out of bed at all, much less went outside.

During this time, I broke up with my girlfriend, a relationship that was important to me. I couldn't talk to her about what was going on with me, much less explain it. It got to the point where I didn't go outside or even answer the phone. I had no social life. My money was running out, and I had no future that I could see. I got more and more depressed, more and more scared.

Finally, my best buddy from came into town. I hadn't seen him for a couple of years. So I actually dragged myself out of bed, cleaned myself up, and met him for dinner. Over a couple of drinks, I found myself telling him what was happening, crying into my beer.

Well, to cut to the chase, the next day, I called a shrink. We talked. He prescribed. We talked some more. I'm still shaky, but better. I still have to force myself to be sociable, but I've got a job interview next week.

Angry at your bully? Good. You should be. Rant away. Expressing anger is healthy, so long as it doesn't translate into violence, whether inwardly or outwardly directed. To channel it appropriately, especially if you harbor any concerns that your anger will urge you to ill-advised action, find yourself a good therapist.

All of the symptoms including mild anxiety, severe panic attacks, sleeplessness, and flashbacks that are listed in Chapter 4, "The Impact of Bullying," are common in the post-bully period. If you're experiencing any of these with any consistency, don't feel shy about seeing a doctor. Therapy and/or medication can be invaluable in getting you back on the right track. And while you may be worried about the expense, it's worth it if you can find someone whom you can trust, who can provide regular reality checks and help you deal appropriately with your understandably volatile emotions. If your doctor is unfamiliar with the dynamics of workplace bullying and the effect on the target's health, appears unsympathetic, or you simply don't feel comfortable with her, change doctors.

Getting back on the road to health and self-confidence may be the single most important thing you can do. It will take time and effort, and you may need some help along the way. But, ultimately, you can and will succeed.

Your priority is doing what's best for you. Depending on your individual circumstances, once you've left your job, you may well feel like a basket case, reluctant to leave the house, talk to people, maybe even to get up out of bed in the morning. Or you may be able to function at normal or near-normal levels.

If you are functioning at top form, that's great—the more power to you. Maybe all you needed was to leave your toxic environment. But perhaps the other shoe hasn't dropped just yet. Once you fully process what you've been through, you could start feeling some of those symptoms.

In any case, one of the most difficult, yet most important, challenges you will face is ultimately putting your anger behind you and dealing with any guilt or shame your bully may have manipulated you into feeling. But you don't have to do it all at once. And you don't need to do it instantly. You're not perfect, and you don't have to pretend to be.

YOU'RE NOT GUILTY

There is no doubt that bullies tend to target those who are vulnerable, those whose childhood and upbringing may have made them more susceptible to being bullied. That does not mean that the targets of bullying are guilty of encouraging the bullying behavior or are in any way responsible for it. But the more you learn about your vulnerabilities and how to deal with them, the more effective you are likely to be in keeping bullies you encounter down the road from taking over your life.

In no way, however, does being proactive in preventing future occurrences let the bully off the hook. Even if you are an easy target, that doesn't make you a willing one. And that's a difficult lesson for both bully and target to learn. If you blame yourself, fighting back becomes difficult, if not impossible. However, understanding the bully-victim relationship can contribute to developing better strategies to challenge it. Of course, it's going to take a while longer to recover, which is all the more reason to start working on it today.

Still wondering if maybe it really is your fault? Maybe you could have tried a little harder to placate your boss? Maybe you could have produced more? Maybe you could have made fewer mistakes? Well, stop it right now. No, you're not perfect. Realize it, and get over it. Your bully depended on his ability to make you feel guilty and ashamed. Don't give him what he wants, even in absentia.

THE NEW JOB SEARCH

If you left your last position because of bullying, your first step will probably be to rally all your emotional resources to face the task before you. You've been battered and bruised by your last job, and now need to put that behind you as you prepare to move on. But before you jump back into the job market, take the time to assess your skills and training, and determine if it's time to apply them in a new way or in a new industry.

If you are or recently were the target of a bully, chances are you've given most of your energy over to surviving the work day. While this is not the place for a detailed discussion of the job market, a brief look at the job hunt is in order (A number of helpful books on changing careers and related subjects are noted in the appendix.).

Picking yourself up, brushing yourself off, and starting on the job search can be an extraordinarily powerful and positive experience. It's a huge step toward regaining control of your life and wresting the last vestiges of power from your bully. Now is the time to shift gears and begin to get reacquainted with your interests and with the skills you most enjoy exercising.

In other words, what makes you happy? What work-related achievements, what activities give you the most satisfaction? What hobbies do you enjoy that might have an application to the working world? Get some new insights into yourself and your goals.

You might start by doing some basic research on career choices of interest to you. Check out resources on the Internet and at your public or local college library. Join professional associations and network with people who are doing what you think you might like to do. Your goal is to know as much about your chosen field as people who have been in it for years.

Once you've done your research, explored different directions, and have reached a decision about the work that suits you best, you'll need to develop a detailed plan that will enable you to make the transition to your chosen career.

If your career change involves additional training, how will you finance it? Explore your eligibility for scholarship and loan programs, as well as apprenticeship programs. Peterson's (www.petersons.com/finaid) is a good place to start for the former; for a guide to apprenticeship and other programs, check out www.khake.com/index.html.

If no formal training is necessary, but experience is helpful, a first step may be to parlay your current profession into a new one. For instance, if you are an accountant by training, but want to own and/or manage a restaurant, perhaps you can edge into the business by doing the books for a restaurant you like. If you've worked in sales or marketing, but running a bookstore is your perfect job, can you help a neighborhood bookstore develop a promotional campaign? Your goal is to leverage your current skills by finding an application for them in the field you've chosen. Ask yourself these three key questions:

1) What do I do best?

2) What do I enjoy doing the most?

3) How can I combine 1 and 2 in the current job environment?

While not essential, a career counselor may be helpful in setting you and keeping you on the right path. Look for a counselor who is certified by the National Career Development Association (NCDA) or another professional organization. For information on the NCDA, visit www.ncda.org on the Web.

If you're looking for a position other than work you've been trained in, overcoming other people's preconceived ideas of what you're capable of achieving may be the biggest challenge you face. However, if you're aware of that difficulty when going into a job interview or pitching yourself to a recruiter, you can overcome this challenge.

But first you want to make sure that the path you choose is indeed promising, and that you have the right personality to make the change and thrive in your new career. Some people spend time in a position in their chosen field on a part-time, temporary, and/or voluntary basis just to develop a feel for its pace and character. You may not be in a financial position to take that route but, at the very least, you should research the area thoroughly. Don't overlook the obvious. You can find information in books, on the Internet, and by speaking with people doing what you want to do.

Become as knowledgeable as you can about the position you're seeking and get as much insight as you can into your prospective employer. Search your personal network for people who know the industry and its players, search the Web for information, study your college alumni directory for former schoolmates who might be able to lend a hand, ask your friends if they know anyone who can help.

Want to be your own boss? If you have an entrepreneurial streak, look into starting your own business. It's hard work, and will likely require some startup capital and lots of initiative, but a business of your own may be the perfect solution for you. See the appendix for some suggested reading on the topic.

If you decide instead to return to the job market, that, too, will take plenty of initiative. Be very clear on how your skills, and experience can be applied to the job you're interested in. Once you land an interview, the better you can articulate how your skills and experience apply, the more enthusiasm you exhibit, the more flexibility you display, the better your prospects are. Your enthusiasm and flexibility can help persuade hiring managers that they will benefit by hiring you, even if you're not a textbook candidate for the job.

Be able to articulate why you want to make a career change. Don't cast it in negative terms, i.e., to get out of an unhealthy situation. Instead look at what draws you to the career you've chosen.

Identify the relevant skills and abilities you possess that can help to sell you in your new career. Talk to friends, your manager, and anyone who knows your work about your strengths, skills, and experiences. Look at old performance reviews for insights into what others perceive to be your strengths and weaknesses, but skip those from your bully. He's done enough. Analyze projects where you succeeded in order to uncover the skills you used to accomplish your task.

As you do your research, match your existing skills to the new job requirements and see what's missing. This exercise will enable you to tailor your resume to suit the position you're seeking and to help you to uncover the skills you'll need to acquire in order to be a competitive candidate.

Identify experience you have that is related to the job you are seeking. For example, if you have experience teaching—whether it's the second grade, beginning French, or auto mechanics—you can translate what it took to be an effective teacher into the parlance of business, e.g., interpersonal skills, managerial abilities, and leadership experience. Similarly, if you want to get into sales, and have dealt with vendors at your last job, you can say you've seen up close what they do and how they do it and you know firsthand what works with customers and what doesn't. Finding and landing the right job is not going to be easy, but it is achievable. And the end result will be far more fulfilling than trying to placate your bully ever was.

As you review your career choices and options, now is also the perfect time to take stock of your job skills. Are there skills you need to brush up on? New ones that would make you more marketable? Check local colleges and universities for classes that can help you move forward in your career.

If, instead, you like the work you've been doing—just not who you've been working for—get started on your job search. During the course of a typical work day, you might want to:

· Call, write, or email job contacts and prospects.

· Search online and print sources for possible job opportunities, both temporary and long term.

· Work on your resume. Write cover letters and follow-up correspondence.

· Find new ways to network, stay in touch with friends and acquaintances in your field, find volunteer or part-time work.

· Keep up to date on your industry. It will help you to stay connected to the work world and ensure that you're not taken by surprise when an interviewer asks you about some emerging industry challenge, product, service, or trend.

· Put your workplace documentation to one side, and start a new journal. Use it as a place to express yourself and your feelings.

REBUILDING YOUR SELF-CONFIDENCE

The more confident you feel, the more likely you are to conduct a thorough job search, do well in interviews and land the right job. Your interviewer will be scrutinizing your attitude as well as your words. If you come to your appointment feeling angry, discouraged, depressed, or nervous, he'll probably detect it.

To help battle the low self-esteem and ebbing confidence that can accompany you when you leave your job, there are a number of steps you can take to boost your morale, and keep it high.

Staying healthy becomes more important than ever when you're facing extra stress, making exercise and good nutrition even more important. In addition, simply ensuring that structure exists in your life and your job search can be a huge help. You may find the going easier if you approach your job search as if it were your work, and break down the various elements into tasks that you can easily accomplish.

To start with, make a schedule for every day and try to keep to it. Be realistic. Don't cram it too full of items you must get done. If you can't face the phone one morning, don't beat yourself up over it. Just don't make a habit of it. Dive back in the next day. If you find yourself surfing the Web or playing solitaire for hours on end, take another look at your schedule. Maybe bulk it up a little or take a thoughtful look at just what it is you're avoiding by perfecting your solitaire game. Maybe you need to fine tune your goals. Or maybe you need some more time or more support before you jump back into the job market.

Take the time to define projects you need to complete, and set deadlines for yourself. Tack your schedule up next to your computer as a reminder. Don't sleep in. Get dressed "for work" every morning. Jeans and a t-shirt are fine. Just get dressed and get going.

Keep in mind that finding the right job can be a long process, and that you'll need to keep yourself motivated, interested, and disciplined. Don't be discouraged if you don't find the right job in a week, a month, even six months. Although easy to say, this last item is tough to do.

15.

THE SECOND TIME AROUND

> One of the awful consequences that I have seen, both as a organizational consultant and a psychologist, occurs when people are suffering so that they are so disabled by depression or anxiety that they become, in effect, ineffective. They cannot look for another job, they can barely get out of bed. If they do get an interview, they show badly and don't get the job.
>
> —*Harvey Hornstein*

You've gotten over the initial hurdles, and have begun to talk seriously about a new job. Make certain you're ready for any curves your prospective employer may throw at you. Be prepared to deal with the issue of references, as well as your reasons for parting company from your last job.

The best way to deal with an abusive manager in your past is to be candid about your experience and your expectations. At the same time, however, your prospective employers may not want to hear about your experience, even though it was abusive, intolerable, and emotionally shattering. They'll most likely only want to know what you will contribute to their company.

Even if your former employer says nothing overtly negative about you, the interviewer may leave with an impression that is less than stellar. Is there anyone at the company other than your bully whom you could list as a reference, such as a manager who preceded your bully or someone from a different department with whom you worked closely?

If you think that the odds are good that a prospective employer is going to talk not just to the references you've listed but to others who might leave a less-than-favorable impression, you may be well-advised to head potential problems off at the pass.

If your job lasted three months or more, your best bet is to explain, as objectively and candidly as possible, your view of what happened. If your last job lasted only a short time—six months or less—you may want to simply drop it from your resume and hope for the best. However, if you choose this route, you run a risk. If a potential employer discovers this gap on his own, your omission may prompt him to wonder exactly what you were hiding and why you were hiding it.

Ideally, as part of the termination agreement you negotiated (See Chapter 13, "Leaving Your Job."), you're the proud owner of a positive letter of recommendation from your previous employer. Don't be shy about handing a copy to an interviewer. Your former employer will need to watch his step if your interviewer should call for more information if he's already on record saying good things about you.

If your former employer did not provide you with a suitable letter of recommendation, don't try to conceal the fact that your relationship with him was less than idyllic. Be straightforward. Tell the new employer that there was a conflict and that, if he should choose to call your old company, a positive referral is unlikely.

By ensuring that a potential employer hears about a negative reference from you rather than from your bully, you can lessen its impact. In addition, should you decide to sue your former employer for defamation, the fact that you felt compelled to explain the circumstances of your departure could, down the line, help to establish that you have been defamed. That is, because you've been compelled to repeat your bully's original false statement about you, he has managed to, through your need to repeat his statements, defame you once again. Keep in mind, though, that you'll need to establish that you believed that you had no choice other than to tell your story. Proving defamation is not easy. Proving that you were compelled to repeat the defamatory comment may be even tougher.

In any case, don't pour out your soul to the interviewer, but—if it comes up, or if you suspect your interviewer will call your old boss—don't be afraid to say that you and he were not the best of buddies. You'll be in a much stronger position if you explain the situation to your interviewer than if you let your old boss have the first word.

Suggest other people at your old company with whom your prospective employer can speak. Make sure you let these references know to expect a call. Update them on any recent achievements and remind them of past accomplishments.

A job interview is not the time to rant about a past boss, no matter how appealing the thought. Instead, confine yourself to statements like "We had dramatically different views on a variety of issues, and were unable to reconcile them."

Be prepared to expand on that statement and to explain what you are doing to ensure that you won't encounter that same problem again. For example, you might say that the reason you have so many questions for your interviewer is that you are very motivated to ensure that the company and you would be a good fit or provide an explanation along the lines of "My management style proved to be very different than that of my former manager. As a consequence, I came to believe that I could not be as effective there as I am capable of being."

Be prepared to describe your management style as well as how it complements the culture of the company with which you're interviewing. For example, you may say that you prefer to manage by motivating people through positive reinforcement and encouraging them to be autonomous while providing them with the resources, support, and guidance that they need.

Then move the conversation back to the job in hand. "Could you tell me more about this position? What exactly are the duties? To whom would I report?" Go on to explain how your skills, expertise, and experience would complement the needs of your prospective employer.

Do tell a prospective employer that your departure was neither whimsical nor arbitrary, but was part of a process during which you came to realize the company was simply not a place where you felt you could develop professionally. You might add something to the effect that, although you felt you had made positive contributions at your former place of employment (be prepared to detail them), after being there for however long, you ultimately concluded it did not and would not provide you with an opportunity to utilize your skills, expertise and experience to the utmost.

THE EMPLOYER'S PERSPECTIVE

Although most employment applications include an employment history section requiring you to explain briefly why you left one place of employment for another, vague responses such as "career change" or "personality conflict" obviously don't tell a prospective employer the whole story. Therefore, as part of the hiring process, employers are increasingly utilizing background checks. While many companies make it a policy not to disclose information beyond the basic details of employment, that is not always the case.

Although a number of states have enacted laws making it difficult for ex-employees to sue former employers for the consequences of reference disclosures, you do have legal recourse if your former employer or one of his agents has made defamatory remarks about you. However, assuming a former employer won't say anything negative about you for fear of litigation can be risky. Many employers will answer detailed questions about a former employee and, if they have an axe to grind, watch out. In many cases, they're protected by law, as long as the information is job-related, based on credible evidence and made without malice. To bypass that protection, you would have to prove that one or more of those conditions did not exist. In Illinois, for example, the 1996 Employment Record Disclosure Act gives qualified immunity to employers who provide negative references. Other states have similar statutes.

The thinking behind this legislation is that an employer has the right to know if the individual he's about to hire stole from his former employer, used illegal drugs at work, etc. But if you discover that you've lost a job offer because of a former employer's reference, you may have the basis for a credible lawsuit if the reference wasn't directly solicited and/or fully accurate.

Former employers who fear potential defamation and slander lawsuits have become crafty when answering employment reference questions. Rather than speak negatively about a former employee, some will opt for a more subtle "no comment" when asked critical employment questions regarding performance, termination, and eligibility for rehire. Also keep in mind that a prospective employer is under no obligation to tell you what he has heard or learned about you.

THE BAD REFERENCE

You thought you had put it all behind you, the bully at work and the trouble he caused. And then, just when you thought it was safe to return to the job market, he strikes—a bad reference that quashed your chances of getting a great new job.

A reference does not even need to be defamatory in order to sabotage your job prospects. A mediocre reference can be enough to derail that job offer. A former employer's tone of voice or a thoughtful pause may be enough to do the trick.

Made cautious by the prospect of defamation suits, most companies don't allow managers to comment on former employees, and instead require them to refer such requests to the human resources department. HR, in turn, typically provides only basic information, confined to a general job description, title, and length of time on the job.

DEFAMATION DEFINED

"An act of communication that causes someone to be shamed, ridiculed, held in contempt, lowered in the estimation of the community, or to lose employment status or earnings or otherwise suffer a damaged reputation. Such defamation is couched in 'defamatory language.' Libel and slander are defamation."
—from The 'Lectric Law Library's Legal Lexicon (www.lectlaw.com)

Your former employer is only permitted to disclose the truthful reasons for your departure, whether voluntary or involuntary, if specifically asked for them without prompting. That means that if your old manager, the HR department, or another agent of your former employer volunteers any information—true or false—to another person or another employer, your employer may have violated the law.

Not only is an employer not allowed to make false statements about your departure, he may not make any type of misrepresentation that prevents or attempts to prevent you from getting a new job. A misrepresentation can be any form of communication—an action, innuendo, or inference that leads the listener to believe something untruthful or misleading about the employee in question. It need not be a direct statement. It could be a gesture, a tone of voice, a facial expression. But proving that your former employer prevented you from landing a job could be tough indeed.

In theory, to prove defamation, you do not need witnesses or external evidence. In practice, making your case is a lot easier if you have confirming evidence, such as a letter, a memo, an email, or the statements of witnesses.

In defamation cases, damages are presumed, so you won't need to prove that the defamatory comments have caused you emotional or psychological harm. Comments do not have to be stated or "published" to someone outside the company. If another employee heard or read the comment then the defamatory statement has been "published" sufficiently to support a charge of defamation.

Most states allow people to sue over bad references if workers can show they have been defamed by their ex-employers. A number of states also have laws that make workplace misrepresentation a crime.

PROVING DEFAMATION

An employer who in good faith discloses information that he believes is true to a prospective employer or other person who has a legitimate interest in receiving the information is probably protected against a defamation suit. This protection may be lost, however, if the information goes beyond the inquiry being made or is disclosed at an improper time or in an improper manner.

Defamation is a general term for a false attack on another's character or reputation. Libel is a type of defamation, generally referring to words in print or misleading and/or deceptive images that expose the subject to hatred, contempt, ridicule, or disgrace; causes the individual to be shunned or avoided; or adversely affects the individual's livelihood.

Similarly, slander refers to defamatory remarks that are

heard, rather than written and that may adversely affect the individual's livelihood.

Defamation is usually characterized by one or more of the following: accusations, exaggerations, malicious speech—that is speech designed to hurt the target—and outright lies.

ACCUSATIONS

Accusations that an employee engaged in illegal or improper conduct often provide the basis for defamation lawsuits. Employers have been held liable for defamation for making statements to the effect that a former employee was a thief, used illegal substances, or made sexual advances to a coworker.

If your former manager tells a prospective employer that you were fired because you abused drugs when you were never convicted of doing so, the statement is likely defamatory. Even if he modifies his remark, saying you were fired because of allegations that you used drugs, the statement still may be defamatory. However, as discussed in this chapter, knowing that a statement is defamatory does not mean you will be able to prove it in a court of law.

EXAGGERATIONS

Employers can also get into trouble by exaggerating an employee's misconduct. For example, a statement that an individual was fired for "gross insubordination" is probably defamatory if the employee's alleged misconduct was trivial or unintentional.

INAPPROPRIATE DISCLOSURES

An employer providing references is typically only protected from defamation if his statements are made to individuals with a legitimate business interest in the information disclosed. Disclosure of details of your termination may be defamatory if made to other employees or friends who have no real need to know specifically why you left.

CARELESS OR FALSE STATEMENTS

If the employer makes statements that he knows are untrue or makes no effort to determine if they are true, those statements are very likely defamatory.

Each repetition of a defamatory remark is a new injury, which means—at least in theory—that you may be able to obtain damages for each time the defamatory statement is repeated. Moreover, if you are compelled to repeat the defamatory statement (in order to explain or rebut it, for example), you may be entitled to receive damages for each repetition. In other words, let's assume that your employer had made a false allegation about you and used it as a pretext to terminate you. Now unemployed, you feel the need to explain the allegation to a potential employer and defend yourself against it. Under these circumstances, because you needed to air the comments in order to defend yourself against them, your repetition of the defamatory comments may itself be considered defamation, for which you are entitled to be compensated.

But, of course, nothing is that simple. In some cases, you or your attorney will need to deal with the issue of "privilege." That is, the defamer may be legally entitled to make defamatory statements in, for example, some judicial proceedings.

In other words, in some cases, statements, that made in other contexts would be defamatory, may be protected under certain circumstances, such as during the course of a judicial proceeding. However, each case is different, so discuss yours thoroughly with your attorney before taking any action.

The employer has the burden of proving that a statement alleged to be defamatory is true. However, to be deemed defamatory, a statement must also seem to state a fact, or appear to be based on fact. An opinion or a statement based on an opinion is not defamatory.

Statements that courts have determined to be defamatory generally involve allegations of embezzlement, lying, irresponsibility, lack of integrity, dishonesty, laziness, incompetence, insubordination, betraying the company, or committing a criminal act. Because proving a defamation case can be extremely difficult, you and your attorney will probably want to explore other options, which means that you may ultimately choose to pursue a retaliation or discrimination case rather than a suit alleging defamation. If your former employer is saying negative things about you to others, then he is very likely damaging your prospects of landing a new job. In addition, you and your lawyer may conclude that those negative statements demonstrate his animosity toward you. Thus, although his remarks may not technically be defamatory, they may offer persuasive evidence that he is violating the laws prohibiting retaliation.

In addition, if you can prove that your employer has violated your right to privacy, provided false information, or has attempted to "blacklist" you, you also may have compelling grounds for a lawsuit.

Keep in mind that such cases are difficult to prove. That's why it's essential that, before you go to court, you and your attorney carefully review the evidence as well as the applicable laws and other factors that may be involved.

INVASION OF PRIVACY

If you believe your employer has disclosed information regarding your personal life, you may have the basis for a suit alleging invasion of privacy. Unlike defamation, truth is not a defense. In an invasion of privacy suit, your former employer can be held liable even if the information disclosed is true.

FALSE INFORMATION

In several states, a former employee can sue an employer who gives false information to prospective employers with the intention of interfering with the former employee's prospects for employment. This type of claim is similar to, and may be filed in conjunction with, a defamation claim. It differs slightly from defamation in that it focuses primarily on the employer's intent.

BLACKLISTING

In a majority of states, "blacklisting"—characterized by Lawyers.com as "malicious action to keep you unemployed"—a former employee is against the law. Blacklisting laws originally were intended to prevent employers from providing negative job references in retaliation for a former employee's participation in a union or other protected labor activity. However, today these laws are generally construed to encompass any communications designed to prevent former employees from securing employment.

REFERENCES, ANYONE?

In a recent survey conducted by the temporary staffing agency Accountemps, hiring managers were asked, "When conducting a reference check, on average, how many references do you call?" Seventy percent said "three" or "more than three." Just four percent said "none."

Most blacklisting laws specifically permit employers to supply letters of recommendation or service as long as the information provided is neither false nor defamatory. In Texas, for example, the law states: "It is unlawful to blacklist an employee in order to prevent the employee from obtaining gainful employment, and to conspire with others to prevent an employee from obtaining employment. However, companies are permitted to provide a truthful written statement about the reasons for termination, and cannot be sued for making a truthful report of problems with the employee."

SO YOU'VE FOUND THE JOB

Okay, so you found a job that looks good. And you want it. But do not let your eagerness overwhelm you or you may find yourself working for a bully again. Now is the time to check out potential problems and to negotiate whatever benefits are important to you. Assess prospective employers just as closely as they are scrutinizing you. Even if the company is one you've always wanted to work for, the position sounds like your dream job, and the benefits are superb, hold on.

Before you accept an offer, look for warning signs, such as unusually high staff turnover, high absentee rates, excessive workloads, rigid bureaucracy, and excessive litigation, mediation, or arbitration. An easy way to get started is to search for the company name along with "lawsuit" or "employment" and see what comes up.

Spend time talking with current employees out of the shadow of the hiring manager or human resources department if you can manage it. Get a feel for the working environment and the corporate culture. If possible, go beyond the department for which you'd be working. Talk to your counterparts in other departments or divisions. Ask yourself if:

· subordinates relate to the boss in a way that you would find comfortable

· your prospective manager listens to what others, especially junior employees, have to say

· the workload seems reasonable and reasonably distributed

Find out all you can about the individual you'd be replacing. Was the person's departure because of a promotion, a transfer, a resignation, or a dismissal? If possible, talk to that individual, or others who have held the same or similar positions, and learn what you can about the position and the management style. If contact information isn't available, check local telephone books, do a Google search on the Web, or use Yahoo!, InfoSeek, or another search tool to get their phone number and/or email. They probably will be willing to speak with you. If they're not, that may tell you something as well.

Keep an open mind. Even in some of the worst job environments, you may be fortunate enough to encounter an excellent manager whose skills, abilities, and personality enable you to work happily and productively. But just as easily, you can get stuck in an abusive situation in even the "best" companies.

LISTENING TO THE SUBTEXT:
WHAT IS NOT BEING SAID

The most important thing you can do when talking to your prospective coworkers is to learn to read between the lines. Even though they may be trying to tell you something, your potential colleagues will rarely come out and say it. As in any interview, keep an ear out for odd hesitations and answers that don't really respond to your questions.

Don't be so anxious to get the job that you neglect or fail to pay attention to your research. Talk to both past and current employees to get a feel for the workplace environment—for example, whether the atmosphere is relaxed and collegial or tense and competitive—as well as the factual components. "Factual" questions may include:

- turnover rates

- predecessor's reason for leaving

- predecessor's length of time at position

- contact info for your predecessor

- performance review history

Subjective issues to look at include:

- morale at company

- reasons for overall turnover

- working environment

- management style

- employee's own level of satisfaction

- how the employee's job differs from how she originally understood it

In addition, consider how the workplace "feels" to you. Ask:

- Is it the type of environment in which you would feel comfortable?

- Do employees seem unusually quiet in the manager's presence?

- Does your prospective manager criticize his staff or past members of his staff in your presence?

- Does your prospective manager talk about others behind their back or interrupt them or you?

SUBJECTS FOR NEGOTIATION

- start date
- base salary
- bonus/incentive programs
- commissions
- telecommuting/business travel
- performance/salary reviews
- signing bonus
- profit sharing
- stock/stock options
- ESOPs/ESPPs
- vesting schedule
- health coverage
- dental coverage
- vision care
- life insurance
- accidental death insurance
- business travel insurance
- short-term disability
- long-term disability
- vacation
- holidays
- sick/personal days
- tuition
- pension plan
- health club membership
- training
- relocation expenses
- dependent care
- overtime
- comp time
- cell phone
- laptop/PDA
- company car
- schedule
- expense account
- parking

THE BACKGROUND CHECK

Unfortunately, your former manager can come back to haunt you, resulting in a negative background check that prevents you from being hired. (For an example of the information available to employers through a background check, see the appendix.) Of course, if he or someone else at your old place of employment is indiscreet enough to say something defamatory, you may have legal recourse.

Similarly, if you have filed a workers' compensation claim, the background check may, depending on local law, provide details on your claim, including the nature of the injury and the disposition of the case.

If you suspect that your former employer is misrepresenting the terms of your departure and/or your employment, or is defaming you, you can use the same service that your prospective employer used, or one like it, to find out exactly what your old employer is saying about you (See the appendix for a partial list.). Compare their accounts to what your prospective employer says. Then get a clear understanding of your expectations and those of your prospective employer. Make sure they match.

REALISTIC EXPECTATIONS OF YOUR NEW JOB

Getting the job offer you were seeking is only the first step, albeit an important one, in your transition. Next, you need to ensure that your expectations match with those of your new employer. For example, will your job be to help make policy, or simply to implement it? What precisely are your responsibilities? How much autonomy do you have, and where does it end? How closely will your manager be supervising you?

Your ability to set the tone for the future is at its greatest before you accept the job offer. Get your job description, responsibilities, and rights in writing, and watch out for the fine (and hidden) print, as well as what is not mentioned at all, i.e., that your employer actually expects you to work seven days a week, or that an employee who voices an opinion different than that of the manager can expect to incur his wrath, or perhaps that the company routinely taps telephone calls for reasons other than ensuring a high level of customer service. Now is the time to make sure that your expectations and those of your future employer are in sync.

In discussing what will be expected of you, make sure that expectations are not only defined but described fully. The more comprehensive the description, the better understanding both you and your employer will have of the goals you are expected to reach, and the tools, time, and training you will need to accomplish those goals.

Make sure you know to whom you'll report and get a sense of that individual's management style, both from the individual and from your prospective coworkers.

THE LASTING IMPACT OF A TOXIC BOSS

Many individuals who quit or are fired because of a bullying boss are so shattered by the experience that they may be unable and/or unwilling to find a new job, according to the Workplace Bullying & Trauma Institute's 2003 Report on Abusive Workplaces. And, in many instances, the incident is likely to have long-term effects on the target's pay as well as on future career prospects.

Other researchers have found that a number of the most severely affected targets will never return to work after leaving a toxic workplace. In some cases, poor health precludes their return. In others, their return is prevented by their inability or unwillingness to deal with potential or perceived conflict.

On a somewhat heartening note, more people are fighting back: According to an ILO report, litigation related to bullying is on the rise.

Understand what's involved in any documents you are asked to sign, including the company's employee handbook. Very frequently, many of these issues are glossed over if mentioned at all. Ideally, they should be explicitly discussed and agreed upon.

Negotiate a termination agreement, including a severance package, in a letter of agreement. The employment agreement may include a clause that mandates arbitration instead of litigation should a dispute ever arise. It and/or the employee's handbook may also provide a definition of "at-will employment."

Your employer may also ask you to agree in writing authorizing the company to speak to past employers. Carefully review, and make certain that you are comfortable with, these and other provisions before signing off on them. If you are not certain about something, you may want to talk with your attorney before signing anything.

An increasing number of companies are asking terminated employees to sign a consent or release permitting them to respond to prospective employers' inquiries or waiving legal claims that might arise from giving references.

JOB INTERVIEW CHECKLIST

· Know exactly what you plan to say about your old job and your bully. Be ready to field questions.

· Be prepared to provide references (make sure anyone you ask to serve as a reference is up to speed with your situation), and have a plan ready if your interviewer wants to speak with your bully.

· Find out in advance what material may appear in a background check and be ready to head off any negative inferences.

Similarly, your prospective employer may ask you to sign a release authorizing entities listed on your employment application to disclose information about you. Make sure that those inquiries will go to the right people. Carefully review the employee manual. Does the employer require that you waive your right to litigation and agree to be bound by an arbitration hearing in case of a dispute? Does the company set down precise standards for your behavior? For that of your manager? Decide before you go much further what is acceptable to you and what is not. If necessary, consult an attorney.

THE IMPORTANCE OF NEGOTIATING

Coming out of a toxic workplace, you may have a low tolerance for anything you perceive as conflict. Don't let that prevent you from negotiating once you've received a new job offer. Yes, you may perceive negotiation as conflict, but you owe it to yourself to get the best deal for yourself that you can. If you don't negotiate at all, you may be at a disadvantage throughout your tenure there.

If you get an offer, get it in writing, and make sure that it includes a comprehensive job description that clearly sets forth your duties, responsibilities, and authority. Review it carefully with your prospective employer to make sure that it means the same thing to you as it does to her.

Make sure your potential manager listens to you when you speak. If he talks right past you now, you'll have little chance of being heard after you're hired.

Respect your instincts. If you have a feeling that you will have a problem if you accept the job, there's probably a good reason for it.

Don't make instant decisions. Consider the offer carefully. In other words, decide in advance what's important to you, as well as where you are willing to compromise. Be sure to negotiate the total package and not just one element, such as salary. Look at the total compensation picture, which includes all of the benefits and perks that are available to you, such as vacation, personal time, paid holidays, health insurance, paid sick time, stock options, retirement plan, IRAs, child care, dependent care, life insurance, tuition support, telecommuting options, flexible hours, stock purchase plans, and any other benefits that are of interest to you. Some points may not be relevant or may not be important to you. Focus on those that are.

GETTING STARTED

When you land your next job, make sure you get started on the right foot. Take an active role in shaping your new position so you won't easily fall victim to a bully. Especially coming out of a toxic work environment, the concept of saying no to unreasonable requests, much less demands, is a tough one to absorb.

As a recovering target of bullying, you're likely to find yourself caught between two extremes. On the one hand, you may have a difficult time trusting an employer (or anyone else), and you may catch yourself being unduly suspicious of people's actions and motives. On the other, you may be anxious to please, to prove to yourself and others that you're a nice person, one worthy of being liked, worthy of being employed.

You'll need to navigate a path between those two extremes. Yes, you want to be perceived as a self-starter, a team player, a conscientious and effective worker with a good attitude. No, you don't want to be a doormat for a bullying boss, losing your life to overtime, making other people's mistakes your emergencies. Some tips for dealing with danger signs are:

· Don't react reflexively if you feel unreasonable demands are being made. Take some time to evaluate what's occurred. If necessary, ask a trusted friend or therapist for a "reality check."

· Be flexible, but don't bend over backward. For example, be willing to work overtime if it's really warranted. Just don't let yourself make a habit of putting in unnecessary overtime.

· Check in regularly with your manager to make sure that your expectations and hers are being met.

· Be open, accessible, and friendly to your coworkers.

· Pause every once in a while and take a look at what you're doing. Are you being overly defensive or, at the other extreme, overly accommodating? If you detect either one or both of these behaviors, take steps to correct them.

· Neither your identity nor your value as a person is determined by how hard you work, much less how many hours you put in.

· Don't be a hero—remember the old line, "Bad planning on your part does not necessarily constitute an emergency on mine." Make those words to live by.

· If you feel your hours are reasonable, but you suspect your manager is not comfortable with the time you are putting in, talk it out before it becomes an issue.

· You're entitled to take a break, to take sick time, to take a vacation. You're entitled to a life.

· Work more efficiently. Get organized, stay organized. Set and keep priorities.

· Not everything needs to be done today, and some of

it can even wait until next week.

· Don't do it all yourself. Delegate and/or ask for help if necessary.

· Just say no. If you don't have time to do it without dropping or delaying another project, say so.

· Temper your loyalty. Before you make your work your life, remember that your company will not hesitate to lay you off if economic conditions warrant.

· Saying no to unreasonable demands and setting boundaries does not mean being abrasive, confrontational, or uncooperative. Try casting your situation as a collaborative process in which you and your manager are seeking ways to help you be more effective.

· If you're sensing that a problem exists, don't work more, harder, or faster and assume that you're addressing the issue. Talk to your manager, and find out what's really going on.

SETTING LIMITS

Unless you are once again working for a bully, reasonable limits that you set will be respected, as you will be respected. If those limits are indeed reasonable, and if your manager rejects them out of hand, then you are working for a bully again. If that proves to be the case, take a look at how the situation evolved, and take steps to prevent it from recurring.

Don't fall prey to an overwhelming sense of guilt, the notion that you need to work late at the office, skip vacations, and eat lunch at your desk. Okay, maybe you do need to put in some overtime occasionally, but not every day, or even every week. If you find yourself falling into this pattern, step back and ask yourself why. Chances are, it's because somewhere in your subconscious, or maybe even in your conscious, resides the fear that if you don't, your boss won't like you, your coworkers won't respect you, and maybe you'll even lose your job.

Stop pushing for perfect. Set realistic standards for yourself. Yes, you want to set high standards, do good work, and move forward with your career, but you don't need to do everything perfectly.

16.

THE NOT-SO-HIDDEN COSTS OF WORKPLACE BULLYING

To state what should be obvious, it's not just the targets of workplace aggression who suffer. Harassment also affects the corporate bottom line.

A bully in the workplace constitutes a huge cost for the employer. Consider the expenses for recruiters, interviewing, training, relocating, advertising, hiring, and yes, firing. Getting a new employee in the door can be an expensive proposition. You'd think that virtually any employer would work to keep a new hire. If you think this, you'd be wrong.

While the costs of are difficult to calculate, there's no question that US businesses lose billions of dollars each year in costs associated with bullying, both directly and indirectly.

THE IMPACT ON PRODUCTIVITY

In a 1998 survey, University of North Carolina management professor Christine Pearson provided some insight into the financial impact of bullying. She found that targets of workplace aggression reported the following:

· Fifty-three percent lost work time worrying about the incident or future interactions.

· Twenty-eight percent lost time at work by attempting to avoid their bully.

· Thirty-seven percent said their commitment to the organization declined.

· Twenty-two percent decreased their amount of effort at work.

· Ten percent decreased the number of hours they put in at work.

· Forty-six percent thought about changing jobs.

· Twelve percent actually changed jobs to avoid the aggressor. [1]

In a separate study, Canada's Respectful Workplace Project in 2002 found that 18.4 percent of those completing its survey had used sick leave as a response to workplace conflict. Just within the commission itself, sick leave in response to unresolved conflict translates into an annual loss of more than $1 million (Canadian). When associated costs—managers' time, EAP-related costs and arbitration recommendations—are factored in, that figure soars to nearly $9.4 million just for that one government agency. [2]

In yet another example, Australia's Beyond Bullying Association cites an Australian study in which 34 percent of bullied victims took time off work as a result of being bullied. The average time taken was 50 days, including 28 days on paid sick leave. In the same study, the group said, nearly one-quarter of those who reported being bullied resigned or retired as a consequence. [3]

The group also cites another Australian study in which more than one-quarter of the respondents reported reduced work output, 22 percent reported an impaired ability to make decisions, and 20 percent reported a decrease in work quality. Finally, increased error margins were reported by 10 percent of those surveyed. Beyond Bullying also cites negative productivity effects on coworkers who witnessed bullying, including bullying-related absenteeism, staff turnover, and productivity. [4]

In the US, work-related diseases including stress account for a total cost of $26 billion annually, according to estimates by the Workplace Bullying & Trauma Institute. [5]

Similarly, in Australia, the Queensland Workplace Bullying Taskforce at Griffith University calculated the hidden costs of bullying at up to $13 billion a year. [6] That survey follows an Australian Council of Trade Unions (ACTU) study of 3,000 workers in late 2000, which reported that 54 percent of workers questioned had experienced intimidation in the workplace, mostly from their supervisors or managers. The ACTU estimated the cost of workplace bullying at $3 billion, reflecting the incidence of physical and mental illnesses, headaches, sleeping problems, and increases in drug and alcohol use.[7]

Stress in the US workplace also represents a major problem, according to the American Institute of Stress (AIS), which estimates that 1 million workers are absent each work day due to stress. The AIS further estimates that stress costs US employers $300 billion a year in absenteeism, health costs, and programs to help workers manage stress.[8]

A LOSE-LOSE SITUATION

Businesses focused on the bottom line have a compelling economic reason to end bullying within the company. Aside from all the emotional and psychological harm that bullying wreaks, it costs businesses a lot of money in the form of:

· reduced productivity

· higher incidence of absenteeism and stress-related leave

· increased exposure to litigation

· lowered morale

· high turnover

· increased training costs

· heightened potential for violence

Although only a fraction of absenteeism due to stress reflects workplace bullying and related issues, that fraction still numbers in the hundreds of millions of dollars, given that an estimated 20 million Americans face workplace abuse daily.

In the UK, Terrence and Dawn Brathwaite, in a paper titled "Confronting Indignity at Work: Comparative Medico-Legal Strategies for Achieving a Just Result," found that an increasing number of employees are losing significant time from work due to stress-related ailments. They estimate that stress and stress-related illness result in the economy losing approximately 270,000 working days every year at an annual cost to UK taxpayers of at least £12 billion.[9]

The stream of numbers continues. A recent survey of 9,000 US government employees found that 42 percent of female and 15 percent of male employees reported being harassed within a two-year period, representing a cost of more than $180 million in lost time and productivity, according to psychologist Michael H. Harrison, PhD, of Harrison Psychological Associates.[10]

Separately, the American Psychological Association has reported that of 1,500 workers surveyed, some 750 said they lost time from work due to rude workplace behavior directed toward them.[11]

In addition to decreased productivity, another negative economic effect of workplace bullying is increased employee turnover, characterized by high replacement costs, including recruiting fees often in excess of 30 percent of the compensation of those hired, overtime pay to those covering job duties, training time for replacements, time expended by trainers, as well as outplacement fees and continued benefits to terminated employees, according to David Bowman of TTG Consultants.[12]

Add to that the potential for numerous lawsuits, stress-related workers' compensation claims, and morale problems, including the negative impact on clients who deal with demoralized employees, and the result should be a compelling economic and human argument for ending workplace bullying.

CORPORATE RESPONSES

So what are US corporations doing about the problem? Not much, it seems, at least not in terms of programs designed specifically to tackle bullying in the workplace.

What can they do? Joel Neuman, who together with his colleagues, has studied bullying extensively at a number of US Department of Veterans Affairs facilities, notes the need to go beyond corporate policies to encourage highly visible leaders within the organization to instill and reinforce the appropriate mindset and "very visibly," deal with violations.

Even more important, he notes, the fundamental nature of human interactions within an organization must change if workplace bullying is to end. Without such a change in the corporate culture, in which employees feel they are trusted, respected, treated with dignity and heard, given some control over their jobs and opportunity to excel, bullying will remain a problem.

Fundamental changes in an organization's mindset can be achieved, but not without considerable effort, education, and expense. If realization of the emotional harm being done to employees and the financial costs to the organization are not enough to motivate fundamental change, perhaps the threat of litigation is.

Writes psychologist Harvey Hornstein at the conclusion of *Brutal Bosses and Their Prey*, "Creating community sanctions to discourage brutality in organizations may seem odious. Ideally, people—bosses included—should voluntarily refrain from injuring one another. But, tragically, they do not. In that case, workers should be able to pursue corrective measures within their organizations.

"Brutal bosses harm communities both at work and beyond by robbing citizens and institutions of their dignity and productivity. These costs cannot be tolerated. Bosses who brutalize subordinates must be outlawed."[13]

17.

LEGAL DIRECTIONS

"Abusive conduct is conduct of an employer or employee in the workplace, with malice, that a reasonable person would find hostile, offensive and unrelated to an employer's legitimate business interests. ... Abusive conduct may include, but is not limited to, repeated infliction of verbal abuse, such as the use of derogatory remarks, insults and epithets; verbal or physical conduct that a reasonable person would find threatening, intimidating, or humiliating; or the gratuitous sabotage or undermining of a person's work performance. ..."

—*Excerpt from California AB 1582*

Little has happened in terms of legal sanctions against bullying since German psychologist Heinz Leymann formally identified the phenomenon in the 1980s. At that time, Leymann estimated that 3.5 percent of all Swedish workers had been victims of a form of harassment he dubbed mobbing, in which one or more coworkers and/or managers target an employee.[1] Subsequently, whether because bullying has grown worse, or employees are more aware of the phenomenon, those rates appear to have risen.

According a 2002 study conducted by Spain's University of Alcal de Henares, 15 percent of workers in the European Union (EU) suffered psychological harassment, or mobbing, on the job.[2] In 1993, to address the issue of workplace abuse, Sweden implemented a measure entitled "Provisions on Measures against Victimization at Work," the first and, of this writing, the only federal legislation to deal with non-specific harassment in the workplace.

Such legislation, however, is under consideration in a number of countries, including Australia, Belgium, Norway, and the UK.

BULLYING AROUND THE WORLD

The following summary of studies provides additional evidence that bullying in the workplace is common worldwide:

Study Author(s)   Leymann, H. & Tallgren, U.
Date of Study   1993
Place of Study   Sweden
Focus of Study   Steel Workers
Percent Bullied   4

Study Author(s)   Kivimäki, M., Elovainio, M., & Vahtera, J.
Date of Study   2000
Place of Study   Finland
Focus of Study   Hospital Staff
Percent Bullied   5

Study Author(s)   Muhlen, Z.
Date of Study   2001
Place of Study   Germany
Focus of Study   Communal Administrators
Percent Bullied   10

Study Author(s)   Trades Union Congress (TUC)
Date of Study   1998
Place of Study   UK
Focus of Study   Telephone Survey
Percent Bullied   11

Study Author(s)   Institute of Personnel Development (IPD)
Date of Study   1996
Place of Study   UK
Focus of Study   Telephone Survey
Percent Bullied   13

Study Author(s)   UNISON (European Trade Union)
Date of Study   1997
Place of Study   UK
Focus of Study   Public-Sector Union
Percent Bullied   14

Study Author(s)   Leymann, H., et al
Date of Study   1993
Place of Study   Sweden
Focus of Study   Nursery School Staff
Percent Bullied   16

Study Author(s)   Bjorkqvist, K.
Date of Study   1994
Place of Study   Finland
Focus of Study   University Employees
Percent Bullied   17

Study Author(s)   Lewis, D.
Date of Study   1999
Place of Study   Wales
Focus of Study   Union Members
Percent Bullied   18

Study Author(s)   Vartia, M. & Hyyti, J.
Date of Study   2002
Place of Study   Finland
Focus of Study   Prison Officers
Percent Bullied   20

Study Author(s)   Keashly, L. & Jagatic, K.
Date of Study   2000
Place of Study   US
Focus of Study   Stratified Random Sample
Percent Bullied   Twelve-Month Period: 27
                      Course of Career: 42

Study Author(s)   Quine, L.
Date of Study   1999
Place of Study   UK
Focus of Study   NHS Trust
Percent Bullied   38

Source: Joel Neuman

Then too, in some countries, the courts are taking a broader look at measures already in place. In Japan, for example, courts have ruled that bullying violates the constitutional right of employees to be treated with respect as well as employers' contractual obligations to provide a safe workplace.

Gradually, legislative action is becoming more effective at tackling the problem of emotional abuse and harassment, and is beginning to address previously overlooked forms of abuse, such as bullying and mobbing.

A 2003 report entitled "Preventing Violence and Harassment in the Workplace," published by the European Community, noted an increasing recognition that workplace abuse consists of behavior that, by itself, may be relatively minor, but which cumulatively can be very serious. Although a single incident can suffice, it notes, "psychological violence" often consists of repeated, unwelcome, unreciprocated, and imposed actions, with an often devastating effect on the victim. The EC defines psychological violence as the intentional use of power against another person or group that can result in harm to physical, mental, spiritual, moral, or social development. [3]

Despite the scarcity of legislation on the topic, the European Community increasingly views bullying, emotional abuse, and mobbing as part of the same phenomenon as harassment related to sexual and racial discrimination. In the 1990s, the European Commission brought together all of these behaviors under a single umbrella, characterizing them as "incidents where persons are abused, threatened, or assaulted in circumstances related to their work, involving an explicit or implicit challenge to their safety, well-being or health." [4]

A July 1999 report by the UK Institute of Management suggested bullying is part of a "new management credo," according to the British magazine *Hazards*. The report concluded that new, leaner business practices are a breeding ground for corporate bullying. [5]

In the US, awareness of non-specific harassment as a workplace issue also appears to be increasing. By late 2003, legislation had been introduced in at least two states that would effectively broaden existing protections to encompass victims of bullying.

California's Healthy Workplace Bill, AB 1582, was the first

measure of its kind to be introduced in the US. In late 2003, the measure's primary sponsor withdrew his support for the bill. However, in the seemingly unlikely event that the measure is passed and signed into law, it would make workplace bullying illegal. Oregon is home to a similar legislative proposal. (For the text of both measures, see the appendix.)

The California bill, introduced in February 2003 by State Assembly members Paul Koretz (D-42) and Gloria Negrete McLeod (D-61), was authored by Suffolk University's David Yamada. In essence, the measure would extend Title VII protections to individuals who have been bullied at the workplace.

BETHANY'S STORY

They [the former employers] are refusing to provide me with a reference. ... Instead they have engaged in subtle blackballing, and are using "implied" statements to future employers, so for now I've given up trying to find a job and have returned to school.

If you think that this is happening to you, talk to your lawyer about the advisability of sending a letter (written by your attorney) to your former employer suggesting that the latter exercise caution before misrepresenting the terms of your departure and/or making defamatory statements.

According to Yamada, AB 1582 represents the first legislative effort in the US that hones in specifically on the problem of workplace bullying. As legislators in other nations, including the UK, are eying measures that would cover much the same ground. "Slowly but surely," says Yamada, "we are seeing the emergence of various legislative and regulatory proposals, usually based on some adaptation of hostile work environment theory or occupational health standards."[6]

This bill would make subjecting an employee to an abusive work environment illegal, and would, under some circumstances, also make the employer liable for abuse committed by its agents.

AB 1582 would also make it unlawful to retaliate against an employee for opposing an unlawful employment practice as defined by the bill or against a worker who has "made a charge, testified, assisted, or participated in an investigation or proceeding under the bill."

Under the proposed law, as a target of bullying, you would be able to file a lawsuit against your employer, alleging emotional distress. You would have the choice of seeking compensation under the bill or filing for workers' compensation, but you would not be able to receive workers' compensation and bring an action under the bill for the same underlying behavior.

As noted, however, the measure has received little support among California lawmakers. Indeed, US legislators overall have been reluctant to enact laws regulating conduct in the workplace. Critics of such legislation argue that the concept of bullying is too amorphous to be regulated by legislation and would lead to a deluge of lawsuits, many of them frivolous.

SANDRA'S STORY

One prospective candidate for my old job found me through an Internet search and emailed me to ask why I had left. I told her, at the same time making very certain not to do anything that could give my former employer a chance to resume bullying me with the threat of litigation. I'm happy to report, she didn't take the job.

For example, the Coalition for California Jobs, which describes itself as a group of "small and large businesses and organizations united to fight anti-jobs legislation and protect and create jobs," claims that the Hostile Workplace Bill would create "a vague new reason to sue employers for harassment."[7]

Critics argue that the measure is unnecessary. Specifically they contend that while cases dealing with managers and supervisors who are abusive may have increased over the past decade, so has the attention that employers have paid to the issue. But, although the expense and bad publicity that employment litigation attracts has been enough to prompt some employers to sit up, take notice, and presumably deal with workplace bullying, there's no sign that the flow of harassment-related litigation is drying up.

The Coalition for California Jobs argues that the measure would "kill jobs" by increasing the costs of litigation, settlements, and insurance and finally that it would "add a new way for aggressive attorneys to profit from frivolous lawsuits."[8] Proponents of anti-harassment legislation, like psychologist Noa Davenport, coauthor of *Mobbing: Emotional Abuse in the American Workplace*, counter that such suits are far from frivolous, and that the impact of bullying can in fact be measured by looking at the tangible harm done to victims. And Yamada argues that, just as sexual harassment is no longer widely tolerated in the workplace, a status-blind cause of action could reduce the harassment and abuse that millions of workers confront today.

Many critics of legislation prohibiting nonspecific harassment suggest that employees who are being subjected to abuse vote with their feet and leave their place of employment. These same folks tend to suggest that, over the long term, employers who countenance abusive managers will not fare well. Though that may be true, it's not of much solace to employees who need a job today and can't afford to walk away from a steady paycheck.

OTHER EFFORTS

Both the California and Oregon measures have something of a precedent in a policy enacted in September 2002, by Oregon's Department of Environmental Quality (DEQ). The department's "anti-mobbing" policy—one of the first such policies in the country—is designed to help ensure a "safe, respectful work environment for all employees, free from mobbing behaviors."[9] DEQ policy states that all employees are expected to adhere to acceptable conduct at all times, including respecting the rights and feelings of others and refraining from any behavior that might be harmful to coworkers.

The policy defines workplace mobbing, which encompasses bullying by managers, as a form of harassment perpetrated by any employee against another employee and which is not based on an individual's protected class status under Title VII, the Americans with Disabilities Act, the Age Discrimination in Employment Act, or related federal laws.

It goes on to further define mobbing as "intentional verbal or non-verbal conduct by one or more individuals against another individual over a period of time," that continuously and systematically:

· intimidates, shows hostility, threatens, offends, humiliates, or insults any coworker

· interferes with a coworker's performance

· has an adverse impact on a coworker's mental or physical well-being

· otherwise adversely affects a coworker

Under this definition, the policy continues, mobbing includes:

· actions intended to physically or emotionally isolate the target

· prohibition of due process

· retribution for pursuing due process

· verbal or physical behavior that is derogatory, abusive, bullying, threatening, or disrespectful[10]

Under the DEQ's policy, the existence of mobbing behavior, or persistent and systematic harassment, is determined based on what a reasonable person would judge to be unacceptable behavior under similar conditions or situations. It defines mobbing as persistent and systematic harassment.

The policy is a result of a collaboration by Local 3336 of the American Federation of State, County and Municipal Employees, and the DEQ. It further defines workplace mobbing as a form of harassment that is not based on an individual's protected class status under legislation such as Title VII, the Americans with Disabilities Act, or the Age Discrimination in Employment Act that is perpetrated by any employee against another employee. It goes on to describe mobbing as "intentional verbal or non-verbal conduct by one or more individuals against another individual over a period of time."

In addition to setting forth definitions and examples of mobbing, the DEQ policy also outlines procedures employees should take to report mobbing as well as the action that the department may take when the policy is violated. Under the policy, "such actions may include but are not limited to, at DEQ's discretion, separating a targeted worker from the perpetrator(s), appropriate disciplinary action, reassignment, and/or mediation by a mutually agreed upon mediator." DEQ policy also prohibits any form of retaliation against an employee filing a good faith complaint under this policy or for assisting in a complaint investigation. If retaliation occurs, it may result in disciplinary action up to and including dismissal of the offender(s).[11]

At present, however, most workers seeking relief for abusive treatment in the workplace not related to one of the protected categories have few other options. Perhaps the most significant option available to them is to file a stress-related workers' compensation claim. However, as discussed earlier, such a step is fraught with problems of its own.

LOOKING AHEAD

In an economic environment where jobs are scarce and states are under pressure to pass pro-business legislation in order to attract and retain employers, passage of effective anti-bullying legislation will be difficult indeed without support from the business community.

Far too many employers today—if they think about it at all—view anti-bullying legislation as anti-business legislation. Ironically, nothing could be further from the truth. As we've seen, such legislation could help businesses increase productivity, reduce downtime and turnover, and boost their bottom line.

Key, then, to ending workplace bullying is educating the business community as well as legislators with regard to the human and economic benefits of ridding bullies from the workplace. Only then will such legislation succeed.

18.

A HAPPY ENDING

To dredge up an old joke, working for an abusive manager is like hitting your head against the wall. Not only do you have about the same level of communication with the wall as you probably do with your boss, but it feels so good when you stop.

Once away from the toxic environment and the bullying boss, and with the support of friends, family, and/or therapist, your life will improve. True, the effects will probably linger for some time. Most likely, it took awhile for them to creep up on you, and it will probably take at least as long for them to fade. And, yes, the memory will remain. But that's not altogether negative. That memory, those experiences, will help you to avoid similar situations in the future, and guide you into healthy working relationships.

Your experience gives you a valuable opportunity to reassess your career, your life, to determine your priorities and set new goals. In my case, for example, I've always been a writer, but for most of my life I wrote on topics that, while interesting, were not a passion of mine.

My bully changed that. Because of him, I have learned that while people's acceptance, respect, and goodwill are important to me, I am no longer willing to go to absurd lengths in my efforts to please them.

I've also learned about the patterns in my life that made me susceptible to a bully, and how to ensure that I avoid similar pitfalls in the future and don't get targeted again. But neither am I healed completely. I still have panic attacks, typically triggered by a fleeting thought or reminder of my bully. However, it's getting better … and so am I.

To some extent, I am more assertive today, less willing to

defer, to placate, to appease. But I still don't like confrontation—I can't imagine I ever will—and I like constantly looking over my shoulder even less. I now have better tools to play that game if I must, but I've also learned that it's as easy to work for a good boss as a bad one, as long as you're able to tell the players apart accurately and quickly.

I am now doing the writing that I've always wanted to do and am beginning to learn, after many, many years, how to stop making work my life and start living more fully.

As I prepared to write this book, I've spoken with many people, and corresponded with more, who have been in situations as bad and often much worse than mine. I am repeatedly struck by how intelligent, articulate, and perceptive so many of them are. Most still bear scars, and likely always will, but they are in various stages of healing and of dealing, of moving on to the next phase of their lives. These are people who are becoming stronger, willing to put the past behind them, able to recognize and deal with the bullies of the future, choosing to take pleasure in their own strengths.

As with any assault—whether physical, emotional, or psychological—there's a temptation to respond by curling up and withdrawing from life. That may be what you need to do, for a time. And that's fine. But then there are those who get stuck, bound up in their experience, bound to the damage that's been done to them. They view the world with suspicion, trusting no one, certain that the world is their enemy. No longer trying to come out the other side.

So keep on trying. It may seem difficult, perhaps even impossible, at times. But you can make it. For that's where the most vital battle lies, not with your bully, but with yourself.

SOURCE NOTES

CHAPTER 3

1. Tim Field interview with author.

CHAPTER 4

1. Seventy-second Oregon Legislative Assembly. "Senate Bill 496."
2. Kate Hoel, et al. "The Cost Of Violence/Stress at Work and the Benefits of a Violence/Stress-Free Working Environment." International Labour Organization. Retrieved May 20, 2004. (www.ilo.org/public/english/protection/ safework/whpwb/econo/costs.pdf).

CHAPTER 6

1. Laura Sofield interview with author.
2. *Sheila E. Horn v. The New York Times.*
3. Steve Murphy interview with author.
4. Ibid.
5. Ibid.
6. Anonymous interview with author.

CHAPTER 7

1. Tom Davison interview with author.
2. Chris Long interview with author.
3. Michael Dubis interview with author.
4. Robin Leonard, Stephen Elias, and L. M. Lawson. *How to File for*

Chapter 7 Bankruptcy and Bankruptcy: Is It the Right Solution to Your Debt Problems? (New York: Nolo Press, 2002), pg. 10.

CHAPTER 8

1. James Stoneman interview with author.
2. Donald Spero interview with author.
3. Paul Buchanan interview with author.
4. Ibid.
5. Ibid.
6. *Thompson v. Tracor Flight Systems.*
7. Ibid.
8. *Shellenberger v. Summit Bancorp.*
9. Cameron Reynolds and Morgan Reynolds. "State Court Restrictions on the Employment-at-Will Doctrine." Regulation: *The Cato Review of Business & Government.* April, 2003. Retrieved May 20, 2004. (www.cato.org/pubs/regulation/reg18n1e.html).
10. Ibid.
11. *Fox v. General Motors Corp.*
12. Spero interview with author.
13. *Bristow v. Daily Press, Inc.*

CHAPTER 10

1. Buchanan interview with author.

CHAPTER 11

1. EEOC.com. "Enforcement Guidance on Reasonable Accommodation and Undue Hardship Under the Americans with Disabilities Act." October 17, 2002. Retrieved May 20, 2004. (www.eeoc.gov/policy/docs/accommodation.html).

CHAPTER 16

1. Christine M. Pearson, "Incivility and Aggression at Work." Envisionworks, Inc. Retrieved May 20, 2004. (www.envisionworks.net/media/incivilityatwork.htm).

2. Heather Comerford. "Respectful Workplace Project." Government of Newfoundland & Labrador. September 2002. Retrieved May 20, 2004. (www.gov.nl.ca/psc/EAP/RWP%20final%20report%20-%20September%202002%20webpage%20version.pdf).
3. Beyond Bullying Association Incorporated. Retrieved May 20, 2004. (cwpp.slq.qld.gov.au/BBA).
4. Ibid.
5. "The US Hostile Workplace Survey 2000." Retrieved May 20, 2004. (www.bullyinginstitute.org/home/twd/bb/res/surv2000.html).
6. Beyond Bullying Association Incorporated. Retrieved May 20, 2004. (cwpp.slq.qld.gov.au/BBA).
7. Australian Council of Trade Unions. "The Workplace Is No Place for Bullying." Retrieved May 19, 2004. (www.actu.labor.net.au/public/resources/bullying).
8. MSNBC.com. "Job stress taking larger toll on US." August 8, 2003. Retrieved May 19, 2004.
(www.msnbc.com/news/950045.asp?cp1=1).
9. Terrence Brathwaite and Dawn Brathwaite. "Confronting Indignity at Work: Comparative Medico-Legal Strategies for Achieving a Just Result." The University of Newcastle, Australia. Retrieved May 20, 2004. (www.newcastle.edu.au/faculty/buslaw/centres_groups/esc/conferen/braithwaite.pdf).
10. Liz Urbanski Farrell. *Orlando Business Journal.* "Workplace bullying's high cost: $180M in lost time, productivity." March 15, 2002. Retrieved May 20, 2004. (orlando.bizjournals.com/orlando/stories/2002/03/18/focus1.html?page=1).
11. Ibid.
12. David Bowman interview with author.
13. Harvey A. Hornstein, PhD. *Brutal Bosses and Their Prey.* (New York: Berkley Publishing Group, 1997), pgs. 148-149.

CHAPTER 17

1. S. Einarsen. "The Nature and Causes of Bullying at Work." *International Journal of Manpower,* Vol. 20 Issue 1/2.
2. Susan Dunn. "An Emotional Intelligence (EQ) Program For Your Employees Can Lower Your Chances Of Being Sued & Lower The Settlement If You Are Sued" InsideOffice.com. August 18, 2003.

Retrieved May 20, 2004. (www.insideoffice.com/insideoffice-20-20030818AnEmotionalIntelligenceEQProgramforYourEmployees CanLowerYourChancesofBeingSuedLowertheSettlementIfYouAre Sued.html).

3. Vittorio Di Martino, et al. "Preventing Violence and Harassment in the Workplace." (Dublin, Ireland. European Foundation for the Improvement of Living and Working Conditions, 2003).

4. Ibid.

5. "Psychoterror: Action is Needed to End Bullying in the Workplace." Sheffield, England: *Hazards*, Fact Sheet 70, 2000.

6. David Yamada interview with author.

7. Coalition for California Jobs. "Coalition for California Jobs Releases Annual 'Job Killer' Bill List." May 29, 2003. Accessed: May 20, 2004. (www.cajobsfirst.org/newsroom_052903.html).

8. Ibid.

9. State of Oregon, Department of Environmental Quality. "Anti-Mobbing Policy No. 50.110. September 19, 2002.

10. Ibid.

11. Ibid.

APPENDIX

I. SAMPLE REPORT: EXECUTIVE LEVEL REFERENCE

KEY:

1=Inadequate
2=Poor
3=Satisfactory
4=Good
5=Outstanding
NC=No Comment
SB=See Below
NP=Not Applicable

Confidential Executive Reference Report

Reference Subject:
Jim Smith

Position Held:
V.P., Sales & Marketing

Dates of Employment:
3/6/97-5/1/98

Reference Checked:
Mr. Cliff Jones

President & CEO
USA, Inc.

Allison & Taylor, Inc. Internal Information:

Date Completed:
7/24/98

Title Confirmed?
Yes

Consultant:
Tiffany Krihwan

Dates of Emp. Confirmed?
Yes

Salary Confirmed?
See Below

Performance Evaluation Questionnaire

Oral Communications:
NC

Financial Skills:
NC

Written Communications:
NC

Technical Skills:
NC

Interpersonal Relations:
NC

Productivity:
NC

Employee Relations:
NC

Decision Making:
NC

Leadership:
NC

Crisis Management:
NC

Short Term Planning:
NC

Personal Integrity:
NC

Long Term Planning:
NC

Overall Performance:
NC

Managerial Skills:
NC

Interview / Correspondence:

[Interviewer:] "Are you able to enthusiastically recommend this person?"

"I'd rather not comment. It's our company policy not to comment on performance or make recommendations on former employees."

[Interviewer:] "Is this person eligible for re-hire within your organization?"

"I wouldn't think so, no."

[Interviewer:] "Could you fully describe the circumstances and reason for the separation?"

"Technically, it was a mutual agreement."

[Interviewer:] "Could you describe any strengths and/or weaknesses of this individual?"

"Again, I'd really rather not comment. According to our agreement I can only confirm the basics."

[Interviewer:] "Would you describe this individual's ability to attract, build, and mentor a team?"

"He was responsible for hiring and managing his sales team."

[Interviewer:] "Could you suggest anyone else that I should speak to regarding this individual?"

"I think you should call Brian Peterson. He's our VP of HR. You can also talk to our Corporate Counsel."

Additional Notes and Comments:

After leaving several messages for Mr. Jones (seven in all), I was finally able to make contact with him after office hours. Please note that at no time did Mr. Jones return my calls. Upon explaining the reason for my call, Mr. Jones agreed to speak with me. His tone was professional although he sounded surprised that I was able to reach him. As Mr. Jones' comments alluded to possible litigation or at least an agreement of some type, I asked Mr. Jones if that were the case. Mr. Jones responded, "I am not at liberty to comment. Please speak with our attorney, Fred Brown."

Source: Allison & Taylor, Inc.

II. FOR FURTHER READING

Biech, Elaine. *The Consultant's Quick Start Guide: An Action Plan for Your First Year in Business*. San Francisco, CA: Jossey-Bass/Pfeiffer, 2001.

Chatzky, Jean. *You Don't Have to Be Rich: Comfort, Happiness, and Financial Security on Your Own Terms*. New York: Penguin, 2003.

Davenport, Noa, et al. *Mobbing: Emotional Abuse in the American Workplace*. Collins, IA: Civil Society Publishing, 2002.

Di Martino, Vittorio, et al. "Preventing Violence and Harassment in the Workplace." Dublin, Ireland: European Foundation for the Improvement of Living and Working Conditions, 2003.

Dobrich, Wanda, et al. *The Manager's Guide to Preventing a Hostile Work Environment: How to Avoid Legal Threats by Protecting Your Workplace from Harassment Based on Sex, Race, Disability, Religion, or Age*. New York: McGraw-Hill, 2002.

Edmunds, Vanessa, et al. *Harassment at Work*. Bristol, UK: Jordans Publishing, 1998.

Fields, Tim. *Bully in Sight: How to Predict, Resist, Challenge and Combat Workplace Bullies*. Oxfordshire, UK: Success Unlimited, 1996.

Hocheiser, Robert. *How to Work for a Jerk*. New York: Vintage Books, 1987.

Hoel, Helge, et al. "The Cost Of Violence/Stress At Work And The Benefits Of A Violence/Stress-Free Working Environment." Manchester, UK: University of Manchester Institute of Science and Technology, 2001.

Holtz, Herman. *How to Succeed as an Independent Consultant, 3rd Edition*, New York: John Wiley & Sons, 1993.

Hornstein, Harvey A., PhD. *Brutal Bosses and Their Prey: How to Identify and Overcome Abuse in the Workplace*. New York: Riverhead Books, 1997.

Hornstein, Harvey A., PhD. *The Haves and the Have Nots: The Abuse of Power and Privilege in the Workplace ... and How to Control It*. Upper

Saddle River, NJ: Pearson Education, Inc., 2003.

Ishmael, Angela, and Alemoru, Bunmi. *Harassment, Bullying and Violence at Work*. Newbury, UK: Spiro Press, 1999.

Kamoroff, Bernard B. *Small Time Operator, 7th Edition*. Willits, CA: Bell Springs Publishing, 2000.

Leonard, Robin. *Bankruptcy: Is It the Right Solution to Your Debt Problems?* Berkeley, CA: Nolo Press, 2000.

Levine, Daniel S. *Disgruntled: The Darker Side of the World of Work*. New York: Putnam Publishing Group, 1998.

Lucht, John, *Rites of Passage at $100,000 to $1 Million+: Your Insider's Lifetime Guide to Executive Job-Changing and Faster Career Progress in the 21st Century*. New York: Viceroy Press, 2000.

Morin, William J., and James C. Cabrera. *Parting Company: How to Survive the Loss of a Job & Find Another Successfully*. New York: Harcourt, 1982.

Morris, Kenneth M. *Wall Street Journal Guide to Understanding Money and Investing*, New York: Fireside Press, 1999.

Morris, Sue. *Sensitive Issues in the Workplace: a Practical Handbook*. Newbury, UK: Spiro Press, 1993.

Namie, Gary, PhD, and Ruth Namie, PhD. *The Bully at Work: What You Can Do to Stop the Hurt and Reclaim Your Dignity On the Job*. Naperville, IL: Sourcebooks, Inc., 2000.

Patsula, Peter J. *Successful Business Planning in 30 Days: A Step-By-Step Guide for Writing a Business Plan and Starting Your Own Business, 2nd Edition*. Mansfield, Ohio: Patsula Media, 2002.

Randall, Peter. *Adult Bullying: Perpetrators and Victims*. London: Routledge, 1996.

Robinson, Joe, *Work to Live: The Guide to Getting a Life*. New York: Berkley Publishing Group, 2003.

III. WEB SITES

ALLISON & TAYLOR REFERENCE CHECKING SERVICES

www.allisontaylor.com

THE ANDREA ADAMS TRUST

UK charity dedicated to tackling workplace bullying.
www.andreaadamstrust.org

ASK THE WORKPLACE DOCTORS

Question and answer forum from communication consultants Dr.
William Gorden and Dan West.
www.west2k.com/wego.htm

BADREFERENCES.COM

www.badreferences.com/index.html

BULLY ONLINE

A project of The Field Foundation, it is one of the world's largest
resources on bullying and related issues.
www.bullyonline.org

EMPLOYMENT LAW INFORMATION NETWORK

A free legal resource site that is designed for employment lawyers, in-
house employment counsel and human resource professionals.
www.elinfonet.com

E-PROREFERENCE

www.e-proreference.com

INSURE.COM

Consumer information on health & disability coverage and

workers' compensation.
info.insure.com

INTERNATIONAL LABOUR ORGANIZATION

A UN agency that seeks the promotion of social justice and internationally recognized human and labor rights.
www.ilo.org/public/english

JOB-LAW.COM

Employee rights Web site.
www.job-law.com

JOBREFERENCES.COM

www.jobreferences.com

MY TOXIC BOSS

Website featuring strategies and resources for targets and victims of workplace bullying.
www.mytoxicboss.com

NATIONAL EMPLOYMENT LAWYERS ASSOCIATION (NELA)

Advocates for employee rights. Provides comprehensive directory of employment attorneys.
www.nela.org

OREGON SENATE BILL 496

www.mytoxicboss.com/oregonlaw.html

PSYCHOLOGICAL ABUSE AT THE WORKPLACE

Published by the University of Adelaide Occupational Health and Safety site.
www.adelaide.edu.au/hr/ohs/occstress/psychabuse/index.html

REFERENCES, ETC.

www.references-etc.com/employment_reference_checks.html

WORKERS' COMPENSATION ADMINISTRATORS DIRECTORY

Comprehensive directory of workers' compensation administrators.
www.comp.state.nc.us/ncic/pages/wcadmdir.htm#dol

WORKERSCOMPENSATIONINSURANCE.COM

Links to Web sites containing information on workers' compensation
issues including forums, law resources, state and federal resources,
fraud, current local and national news and reform efforts.
www.workerscompensationinsurance.com/workers_compensa-
tion/links.htm

WORKPLACE BULLYING AND TRAUMA INSTITUTE

Gary and Ruth Namie's site on bullying research and education.
www.bullyinginstitute.org

WORKPLACE FAIRNESS

Legal issues and resources related to fairness in the workplace
and advocacy to end psychological violence at work.
www.workplacefairness.org

YAHOO! EMOTIONAL ABUSE GROUP

A group dedicated to victims of emotional abuse.
groups.yahoo.com/group/emotionalabuse

YAHOO! TOXIC MANAGERS GROUP

A group devoted to discussion, research, and support related to
workplace bullying.
groups.yahoo.com/group/toxicmanagers

IV. THE US EQUAL EMPLOYMENT OPPORTUNITY COMMISSION: FEDERAL LAWS PROHIBITING JOB DISCRIMINATION: QUESTIONS AND ANSWERS

FEDERAL EQUAL EMPLOYMENT OPPORTUNITY (EEO) LAWS

I. WHAT ARE THE FEDERAL LAWS PROHIBITING JOB DISCRIMINATION?

· Title VII of the Civil Rights Act of 1964 (Title VII), which prohibits employment discrimination based on race, color, religion, sex, or national origin.

· The Equal Pay Act of 1963 (EPA), which protects men and women who perform substantially equal work in the same establishment from sex-based wage discrimination.

· The Age Discrimination in Employment Act of 1967 (ADEA), which protects individuals who are 40 years of age or older.

· Title I and Title V of the Americans with Disabilities Act of 1990 (ADA), which prohibit employment discrimination against qualified individuals with disabilities in the private sector, and in state and local governments.

· Sections 501 and 505 of the Rehabilitation Act of 1973, which prohibit discrimination against qualified individuals with disabilities who work in the federal government.

· The Civil Rights Act of 1991, which, among other things, provides monetary damages in cases of intentional employment discrimination.

The US Equal Employment Opportunity Commission (EEOC) enforces all of these laws. EEOC also provides oversight and coordination of all federal equal employment opportunity regulations, practices, and policies.

Other federal laws, not enforced by EEOC, also prohibit discrimination and reprisal against federal employees and applicants. The Civil Service Reform Act of 1978 (CSRA) contains a number of prohibitions, known as prohibited personnel practices, which are designed to promote overall fairness in federal personnel actions. The CSRA prohibits any employee who has authority to take certain personnel actions from discriminating for or against employees or applicants for employment on the bases of race, color, national origin, religion, sex, age, or disability. It also provides that certain personnel actions can not be based on attributes or conduct that do not adversely affect employee performance, such as marital status and political affiliation. The Office of Personnel Management (OPM) has interpreted the prohibition of discrimination based on conduct to include discrimination based on sexual orientation. The CSRA also prohibits reprisal against federal employees or applicants for whistle-blowing, or for exercising an appeal, complaint, or grievance right. The CSRA is enforced by both the Office of Special Counsel (OSC) and the Merit Systems Protection Board (MSPB).

Additional information about the enforcement of the CSRA may be found on the OPM website at: www.opm.gov/er/address2/guide01.htm; from OSC at (202) 653-7188 or at www.osc.gov; and from MSPB at (202) 653-6772 or at www.mspb.gov.

DISCRIMINATORY PRACTICES

II. WHAT DISCRIMINATORY PRACTICES ARE PROHIBITED BY THESE LAWS?

Under Title VII, the ADA and the ADEA, it is illegal to discriminate in any aspect of employment, including:

- hiring and firing

- compensation, assignment, or classification of employees

- transfer, promotion, layoff, or recall

- job advertisements

- recruitment

- testing

- use of company facilities

- training and apprenticeship programs

- fringe benefits

- pay, retirement plans, and disability leave

- other terms and conditions of employment

Discriminatory practices under these laws also include:

- Harassment on the basis of race, color, religion, sex, national origin, disability, or age.

- Retaliation against an individual for filing a charge of discrimination, participating in an investigation, or opposing discriminatory practices.

- Employment decisions based on stereotypes or assumptions about the abilities, traits, or performance of individuals of a certain sex, race, age, religion, or ethnic group, or individuals with disabilities.

- Denying employment opportunities to a person because of marriage to, or association with, an individual of a particular race, religion, national origin, or an individual with a disability. Title VII also prohibits discrimination because of participation in schools or places of worship associated with a particular racial, ethnic, or religious group.

Employers are required to post notices to all employees advising them of their rights under the laws EEOC enforces and their right to be free from retaliation. Such notices must be accessible, as needed, to persons with visual or other disabilities that affect reading.

Note: Many states and municipalities also have enacted protections against discrimination and harassment based on sexual orientation, status as a parent, marital status and political affiliation. For information, please contact the EEOC District Office nearest you.

III. WHAT OTHER PRACTICES ARE DISCRIMINATORY UNDER THESE LAWS?

TITLE VII

Title VII prohibits not only intentional discrimination, but also practices that have the effect of discriminating against individuals because of their race, color, national origin, religion, or sex.

NATIONAL ORIGIN DISCRIMINATION

· It is illegal to discriminate against an individual because of birthplace, ancestry, culture, or linguistic characteristics common to a specific ethnic group.

· A rule requiring that employees speak only English on the job may violate Title VII unless an employer shows that the requirement is necessary for conducting business. If the employer believes such a rule is necessary, employees must be informed when English is required and the consequences for violating the rule.

The Immigration Reform and Control Act (IRCA) of 1986 requires employers to assure that employees hired are legally authorized to work in the US. However, an employer who requests employment verification only for individuals of a particular national origin, or individuals who appear to be or sound foreign, may violate both Title VII and IRCA; verification must be obtained from all applicants and employees. Employers who impose citizenship requirements or give preferences to US citizens in hiring or employment opportunities also may violate IRCA.

Additional information about IRCA may be obtained from the Office of Special Counsel for Immigration-Related Unfair Employment Practices at 1-800-255-7688 (voice), 1-800-237-2515 (TTY for employees/applicants) or 1-800-362-2735 (TTY for employers) or at www.usdoj.gov/crt/osc.

RELIGIOUS ACCOMMODATION

· An employer is required to reasonably accommodate the religious belief of an employee or prospective employee, unless doing so would impose an undue hardship.

SEX DISCRIMINATION

Title VII's broad prohibitions against sex discrimination specifically cover:

· Sexual Harassment: This includes practices ranging from direct requests for sexual favors to workplace conditions that create a hostile environment for persons of either gender, including same sex harassment. (The "hostile environment" standard also applies to harassment on the bases of race, color, national origin, religion, age, and disability.)

· Pregnancy Based Discrimination: Pregnancy, childbirth, and related medical conditions must be treated in the same way as other temporary illnesses or conditions.

Additional rights are available to parents and others under the Family and Medical Leave Act (FMLA), which is enforced by the US Department of Labor. For information on the FMLA, or to file an FMLA complaint, individuals should contact the nearest office of the Wage and Hour Division, Employment Standards Administration, US Department of Labor. The Wage and Hour Division is listed in most telephone directories under US Government, Department of Labor or at www.dol.gov/esa/public/whd_org.htm.

AGE DISCRIMINATION IN EMPLOYMENT ACT

The ADEA's broad ban against age discrimination also specifically prohibits:

· Statements or specifications in job notices or advertisements of age preference and limitations. An age limit may only be specified in the rare circumstance where age has been proven to be a bona fide occupational qualification (BFOQ).

· Discrimination on the basis of age by apprenticeship programs, including joint labor-management apprenticeship programs.

· Denial of benefits to older employees. An employer may reduce benefits based on age only if the cost of providing the reduced benefits to older workers is the same as the cost of providing benefits to younger workers.

EQUAL PAY ACT

The EPA prohibits discrimination on the basis of sex in the payment of wages or benefits, where men and women perform work of similar skill, effort, and responsibility for the same employer under similar working conditions.

Note that:

· employers may not reduce wages of either sex to equalize pay between men and women

· a violation of the EPA may occur where a different wage was/is paid to a person who worked in the same job before or after an employee of the opposite sex

· a violation may also occur where a labor union causes the employer to violate the law

TITLES I AND V OF THE AMERICANS WITH DISABILITIES ACT

The ADA prohibits discrimination on the basis of disability in all employment practices. It is necessary to understand several important ADA definitions to know who is protected by the law and what constitutes illegal discrimination:

INDIVIDUAL WITH A DISABILITY

An individual with a disability under the ADA is a person who has a physical or mental impairment that substantially limits one or more major life activities, has a record of such an impairment, or is regarded as having such an impairment. Major life activities are activities that an average person can perform with little or no difficulty such as walking, breathing, seeing, hearing, speaking, learning, and working.

QUALIFIED INDIVIDUAL WITH A DISABILITY

A qualified employee or applicant with a disability is someone who satisfies skill, experience, education, and other job-related requirements of the position held or desired, and who, with or without reasonable accommodation, can perform the essential functions of that position.

REASONABLE ACCOMMODATION

Reasonable accommodation may include, but is not limited to, making existing facilities used by employees readily accessible to and usable by persons with disabilities; job restructuring; modification of work schedules; providing additional unpaid leave; reassignment to a vacant position; acquiring or modifying equipment or devices; adjusting or modifying examinations, training materials, or policies; and providing qualified readers or interpreters. Reasonable accommodation may be necessary to apply for a job, to perform job functions, or to enjoy the benefits and privileges of employment that are enjoyed by people without disabilities. An employer is not required to lower production standards to make an accommodation. An employer generally is not obligated to provide personal use items such as eyeglasses or hearing aids.

UNDUE HARDSHIP

An employer is required to make a reasonable accommodation to a qualified individual with a disability unless doing so would impose an undue hardship on the operation of the employer's business. Undue hardship means an action that requires significant difficulty or expense when considered in relation to factors such as a business' size, financial resources, and the nature and structure of its operation.

PROHIBITED INQUIRIES AND EXAMINATIONS

Before making an offer of employment, an employer may not ask job applicants about the existence, nature, or severity of a disability. Applicants may be asked about their ability to perform job functions. A job offer may be conditioned on the results of a medical examination, but only if the examination is required for all entering employees in the same job category. Medical examinations of employees must be job-related and consistent with business necessity.

DRUG AND ALCOHOL USE

Employees and applicants currently engaging in the illegal use of drugs are not protected by the ADA when an employer acts on the basis of such use. Tests for illegal use of drugs are not considered medical examinations and, therefore, are not subject to the ADA's restrictions on medical examinations. Employers may hold individuals who are illegally using drugs and individuals with alcoholism to the same standards of performance as other employees.

THE CIVIL RIGHTS ACT OF 1991

The Civil Rights Act of 1991 made major changes in the federal laws against employment discrimination enforced by EEOC. Enacted in part to reverse several Supreme Court decisions that limited the rights of persons protected by these laws, the Act also provides additional protections. The Act authorizes compensatory and punitive damages in cases of intentional discrimination, and provides for obtaining attorneys' fees and the possibility of jury trials. It also directs the EEOC to expand its technical assistance and outreach activities.

IV. WHICH EMPLOYERS AND OTHER ENTITIES ARE COVERED BY THESE LAWS?

Title VII and the ADA cover all private employers, state and local governments, and education institutions that employ 15 or more individuals. These laws also cover private and public employment agencies, labor organizations, and joint labor management committees controlling apprenticeship and training.

The ADEA covers all private employers with 20 or more employees, state and local governments (including school districts), employment agencies and labor organizations.

The EPA covers all employers who are covered by the Federal Wage and Hour Law (the Fair Labor Standards Act). Virtually all employers are subject to the provisions of this Act.

Title VII, the ADEA, and the EPA also cover the federal government. In addition, the federal government is covered by Sections 501 and 505 of the Rehabilitation Act of 1973, as amended, which incorporate the requirements of the ADA. However, different procedures are used for processing complaints of federal discrimination. For more information on how to file a complaint of federal discrimination, contact the EEO office of the federal agency where the alleged discrimination occurred.

The CSRA (not enforced by EEOC) covers most federal agency employees except employees of a government corporation, the Federal Bureau of Investigation, the Central Intelligence Agency, the Defense Intelligence Agency, the National Security Agency, and as determined by the President, any executive agency or unit thereof, the principal function of which is the conduct of foreign intelligence or counterintelligence activities, or the General Accounting Office.

THE EEOC'S CHARGE PROCESSING PROCEDURES

Federal employees or applicants for employment should see the fact sheet about Federal Sector Equal Employment Opportunity Complaint Processing.

V. WHO CAN FILE A CHARGE OF DISCRIMINATION?

· Any individual who believes that his or her employment rights have been violated may file a charge of discrimination with EEOC.

· In addition, an individual, organization, or agency

may file a charge on behalf of another person in order to protect the aggrieved person's identity.

VI. HOW IS A CHARGE OF DISCRIMINATION FILED?

·   A charge may be filed by mail or in person at the nearest EEOC office. Individuals may consult their local telephone directory (US Government listing) or call 1-800-669-4000 (voice) or 1-800-669-6820 (TTY) to contact the nearest EEOC office for more information on specific procedures for filing a charge.

·   Individuals who need an accommodation in order to file a charge (e.g., sign language interpreter, print materials in an accessible format) should inform the EEOC field office so appropriate arrangements can be made.

·   Federal employees or applicants for employment should see the fact sheet about Federal Sector Equal Employment Opportunity Complaint Processing.

VII. WHAT INFORMATION MUST BE PROVIDED TO FILE A CHARGE?

·   the complaining party's name, address, and telephone number

·   the name, address, and telephone number of the respondent employer, employment agency, or union that is alleged to have discriminated, and number of employees (or union members), if known

·   a short description of the alleged violation (the event that caused the complaining party to believe that his or her rights were violated)

·   the date(s) of the alleged violation(s)

·   federal employees or applicants for employment

should see the fact sheet about Federal Sector Equal Employment Opportunity Complaint Processing

VIII. WHAT ARE THE TIME LIMITS FOR FILING A CHARGE OF DISCRIMINATION?

All laws enforced by EEOC, except the Equal Pay Act, require filing a charge with EEOC before a private lawsuit may be filed in court. There are strict time limits within which charges must be filed:

· A charge must be filed with EEOC within 180 days from the date of the alleged violation, in order to protect the charging party's rights.

· This 180-day filing deadline is extended to 300 days if the charge also is covered by a state or local anti-discrimination law. For ADEA charges, only state laws extend the filing limit to 300 days.

· These time limits do not apply to claims under the Equal Pay Act, because under that Act persons do not have to first file a charge with EEOC in order to have the right to go to court. However, since many EPA claims also raise Title VII sex discrimination issues, it may be advisable to file charges under both laws within the time limits indicated.

· To protect legal rights, it is always best to contact EEOC promptly when discrimination is suspected.

· Federal employees or applicants for employment should see the fact sheet about Federal Sector Equal Employment Opportunity Complaint Processing.

IX. WHAT AGENCY HANDLES A CHARGE THAT IS ALSO COVERED BY STATE OR LOCAL LAW?

Many states and localities have anti-discrimination laws and agencies responsible for enforcing those laws. EEOC refers to these agencies as "Fair Employment Practices Agencies (FEPAs)." Through the use of "work sharing agreements," EEOC and the FEPAs avoid duplication of effort while at the same time ensuring that a charging party's rights are protected under both federal and state law.

· If a charge is filed with a FEPA and is also covered by federal law, the FEPA "dual files" the charge with EEOC to protect federal rights. The charge usually will be retained by the FEPA for handling.

· If a charge is filed with EEOC and also is covered by state or local law, EEOC "dual files" the charge with the state or local FEPA, but ordinarily retains the charge for handling.

X. WHAT HAPPENS AFTER A CHARGE IS FILED WITH EEOC?

The employer is notified that the charge has been filed. From this point there are a number of ways a charge may be handled:

· A charge may be assigned for priority investigation if the initial facts appear to support a violation of law. When the evidence is less strong, the charge may be assigned for follow up investigation to determine whether it is likely that a violation has occurred.

· EEOC can seek to settle a charge at any stage of the investigation if the charging party and the employer express an interest in doing so. If settlement efforts are not successful, the investigation continues.

· In investigating a charge, EEOC may make written requests for information, interview people, review documents, and, as needed, visit the facility where the alleged discrimination occurred. When the investigation is complete, EEOC will discuss the evidence with the charging party or employer, as appropriate.

· The charge may be selected for EEOC's mediation program if both the charging party and the employer express an interest in this option. Mediation is offered as an alternative to a lengthy investigation. Participation in the mediation program is confidential, voluntary, and requires consent from both charging party and employer. If mediation is unsuccessful, the charge is returned for investigation.

· A charge may be dismissed at any point if, in the agency's best judgment, further investigation will not establish a violation of the law. A charge may be dismissed at the time it is filed, if an initial in-depth interview does not produce evidence to support the claim. When a charge is dismissed, a notice is issued in accordance with the law which gives the charging party 90 days in which to file a lawsuit on his or her own behalf.

· Federal employees or applicants for employment should see the fact sheet about Federal Sector Equal Employment Opportunity Complaint Processing.

XI. HOW DOES EEOC RESOLVE DISCRIMINATION CHARGES?

· If the evidence obtained in an investigation does not establish that discrimination occurred, this will be explained to the charging party. A required notice is then issued, closing the case and giving the charging party 90 days in which to file a lawsuit on his or her own behalf.

· If the evidence establishes that discrimination has occurred, the employer and the charging party will be informed of this in a letter of determination that explains the finding. EEOC will then attempt conciliation with the employer to develop a remedy for the discrimination.

· If the case is successfully conciliated, or if a case has earlier been successfully mediated or settled, neither EEOC nor the charging party may go to court unless the conciliation, mediation, or settlement agreement is not honored.

· If EEOC is unable to successfully conciliate the case,

the agency will decide whether to bring suit in federal court. If EEOC decides not to sue, it will issue a notice closing the case and giving the charging party 90 days in which to file a lawsuit on his or her own behalf. In Title VII and ADA cases against state or local governments, the Department of Justice takes these actions.

· Federal employees or applicants for employment should see the fact sheet about Federal Sector Equal Employment Opportunity Complaint Processing.

XII. WHEN CAN AN INDIVIDUAL FILE AN EMPLOYMENT DISCRIMINATION LAWSUIT IN COURT?

A charging party may file a lawsuit within 90 days after receiving a notice of a "right to sue" from EEOC, as stated above. Under Title VII and the ADA, a charging party also can request a notice of "right to sue" from EEOC 180 days after the charge was first filed with the Commission, and may then bring suit within 90 days after receiving this notice. Under the ADEA, a suit may be filed at any time 60 days after filing a charge with EEOC, but not later than 90 days after EEOC gives notice that it has completed action on the charge.

Under the EPA, a lawsuit must be filed within two years (three years for willful violations) of the discriminatory act, which in most cases is payment of a discriminatory lower wage.

Federal employees or applicants for employment should see the fact sheet about Federal Sector Equal Employment Opportunity Complaint Processing.

XIII. WHAT REMEDIES ARE AVAILABLE WHEN DISCRIMINATION IS FOUND?

The "relief" or remedies available for employment discrimination, whether caused by intentional acts or by practices that have a discriminatory effect, may include:

- back pay
- hiring
- promotion
- reinstatement
- front pay
- reasonable accommodation
- other actions that will make an individual "whole" (in the condition s/he would have been but for the discrimination)

Remedies also may include payment of:

- attorneys' fees
- expert witness fees
- court costs

Under most EEOC-enforced laws, compensatory and punitive damages also may be available where intentional discrimination is found. Damages may be available to compensate for actual monetary losses, for future monetary losses, and for mental anguish and inconvenience. Punitive damages also may be available if an employer acted with malice or reckless indifference. Punitive damages are not available against the federal, state or local governments.

In cases concerning reasonable accommodation under the ADA, compensatory or punitive damages may not be awarded to the charging party if an employer can demonstrate that "good faith" efforts were made to provide reasonable accommodation.

An employer may be required to post notices to all employees addressing the violations of a specific charge and advising them of their rights under the laws EEOC enforces and their right to be free from retaliation. Such notices must be accessible, as needed, to persons with visual or other disabilities that affect reading.

The employer also may be required to take corrective or preventive actions to cure the source of the identified discrimination and minimize the chance of its recurrence, as well as discontinue the specific discriminatory practices involved in the case.

V. SAMPLE WORKPLACE JOURNAL

Date	Time	Content of Incident	Medium	My Response	Witnesses	Notes
9/25	10 A.M.	Bob wanted to know why I was late in submitting a memo; said that tardiness was "not acceptable."	Voicemail	Finished the memo and sent it; no direct response.	None	Got very nervous, anxious.
9/25	1 P.M.	Bob yelled at me for not carrying out an errand I had considered trivial; told me I was not to prioritize my agenda, but just do what I was told.	Weekly Management Meeting	Completed errand; sent him memo advising him of its completion; also noted that I would like to meet with him to discuss my job responsibilities.	Shelly, Jack and Kate	They were very, very quiet; I felt shocked.
9/26	9 A.M.	Bob told me I needed to learn how to prioritize on my own; that was part of my job and that he didn't have time to meet with me.	E-mail	Responded by e-mail that I understood from his message that he was too busy to meet with me, and told him that I would do my best to set priorities. However, given that it appeared my job description was changing, I still felt a meeting, at his convenience, to clarify would be helpful.	None	Nervous.
9/28	11 A.M	I found out from Elaine that Bob had told her not to make the calls that I had requested she make.	Conversation with Elaine	Left a memo in Bob's inbox relaying what Elaine had told me, and requesting that he clarify for me what the issue was here.	Elaine	I'm stunned; Elaine is supposed to be my administrative assistant.

INDEX